GOOD VIBRATIONS

Evelyn Glennie was born in Aberdeen in 1965. She started to lose her hearing at the age of 8, and by the age of 12 was profoundly deaf. It was only after this that she took up percussion, and in 1982 went to the Royal Academy of Music to study Timpani/Percussion and Piano. Three outstanding years as a student culminated in being awarded the prestigious Shell/LSO Gold Medal for Percussion and Piano. Her professional career has so far included worldwide tours and the honour of a solo concert in the 1989 Proms, as well as recording her first albums to critical acclaim.

GOOD VIBRATIONS

AN AUTOBIOGRAPHY

Evelyn Glennie

ARROW BOOKS

Arrow Books Limited
20 Vauxhall Bridge Road, London SW1V 2SA

An imprint of the Random Century Group

London Melbourne Sydney Auckland
Johannesburg and agencies throughout
the world

First published in Great Britain by Hutchinson, 1990
Arrow edition 1991

3 5 7 9 10 8 6 4 2

Phototypeset by Input Typesetting Ltd, London
Printed and bound in Great Britain by
Cox & Wyman Ltd, Reading, Berkshire

ISBN 0 09 985120 2

'Who can refuse to live her own life?'
Anna Akhmatova

Contents

Acknowledgements

I should like to thank the following people for their support and encouragement during the preparation of this book: my parents Isobel and Arthur Glennie, and my brothers Roger and Colin; Mr Hamish Park and Mr Alan Cameron of Ellon Academy; Mrs Sandra Merrilees; Ron Forbes; Sandra Buchan; Dr Lionel Naftalin; Ann and Ezra Rachlin; Nicholas Cole, Graeme Humphrey and David Robinson of the Royal Academy of Music; James Blades and his wife Joan; Jasper Parrott, Linda Marks and Sarah Dyckhoff of Harrison/Parrott; Chris Hunt of Iambic Productions; Ronnie Cass, who kindly allowed me to use his memoir of the Shell-LSO competition.

At Hutchinson, I'd like to thank Kate Mosse, my editor, who deserves special gratitude and thanks for encouraging me to write the book in the first place, and for working with me in the early stages. Clare Summerfield and Eva Daniels coped with the burden of typing. I owe particular thanks to Pamela Norris, who developed the manuscript from my drafts, diaries and scrapbooks, and hours of conversation together.

Illustration Acknowledgements

The publishers would like to thank the following for their kind permission to reproduce the photographs that appear in this book:

© Newcastle Chronicle & Journalist Ltd; © the UP Group; © Professional Photographic Services; © Osprey Photography; © Reg Wilson; © Aberdeen Journal Ltd; © the People's Journal; © Times Newspapers Ltd; © BBC; © Barry Swaebe; © Suzie E. Maeder; © Ron Massey.

Whilst every attempt has been made to trace copyright, this has not been possible in some cases. The publishers would like to apologise in advance for any inconvenience this might cause.

Foreword

Writing an autobiography at the age of 24 may seem a little premature. My motive has been simply to set on record the story of how I came to be a musician despite the apparently major disability of being profoundly deaf. I am so often asked to explain both the steps along the way and how I manage to 'hear' music; it seemed a good idea to tell the tale in my own words. Being deaf has of course been very important; I have had to develop my own ways of coping with many things that hearing people take for granted. In particular, in musical terms it has meant finding new ways of responding to music, and also a certain amount of having to fight against prejudice or natural hesitancy by people in the musical world about my ability to cope as a musician. I hope that *Good Vibrations* will show that it is possible to succeed with one's ambitions, despite apparently almost insurmountable obstacles.

Because I am so young this is essentially a musical autobiography. It is a little early for me to have had more than a young woman's first experience of the world, and my life to date has centred around people, places and events in the musical world. Readers may be disappointed at the absence of intimate personal details; they will just have to wait another twenty years until I have had time to live a little more!

Being physically rather small and also female, the first question that everyone asks me is 'Why percussion? Isn't it a man's instrument?' I don't have a satisfactory answer. I encountered no exceptional musical sounds during upbringing on a farm in north-east Scotland and I can only think that curiosity drew my attention to what I soon discovered is an enormous family of instruments. Percussion doesn't just consist of a xylophone as I first thought; add over another 599 objects that can be struck, shaken, rattled and squeezed, and you have a clearer idea of its range. Like any human family, percussion has its ups and downs, but the end result is always communication. Being able to talk to people through music is a great happiness, but I haven't achieved this on my own. The faith, love and stamina of my family, friends and colleagues, and the simple but heartwarming incidents of everyday life have been a tremendous support. Thanks to everyone – and keep in tune!

1

'You have made history'

Late in the evening on 27 July 1989, a packed audience at Kensington Town Hall was eagerly awaiting a unique event in the world of classical music – the first solo percussion recital ever held in the ninety-five years of the BBC's prestigious Henry Wood Promenade Concerts.

There had been tremendous publicity for the event over the previous few days and, as the final call came to take our places on stage, my piano accompanist Philip Smith confessed that much as he had been looking forward to the performance, he would be relieved when it was over. I sympathized, but my emotions were rather different. This was what I had been working for during years of effort to achieve recognition as a solo percussionist; I was going to enjoy every moment and give everything I had to the music. Now, if ever, I would be playing from the heart.

The recital was a sell-out, the first time it had happened for this hall, and people were standing at the back of the auditorium as well as the promenaders crowding in front of the stage. The air was electric with expectation as I walked out to greet the audience and take my place in front of the array of percussion instruments on the platform. I had agreed with the BBC who were broadcasting the event live on Radio 3 that I would, unusually, announce my own programme. Quietly I waited till all eyes were turned towards me; a little pause to prepare us for the music ahead, and then we were away, the trilling notes of a Chopin study adapted for marimba and piano providing a gentle warm up for a programme that ranged from virtuoso fireworks to the sobbing melodies of *Michi*, an exquisite Japanese work that explores and celebrates the pain of unrequited love.

The recital had been planned for many months. I had always wanted to give my own Promenade concert, but there was no tradition for solo percussion recitals in serious music in Great Britain – not, that is, until I embarked on my one-woman crusade to create a wider audience for percussion music. Although there are well over 600 separate and fascinating instruments in the percussion family, the range of compositions for percussion has been comparatively small. For the organizers of the Promenade concerts, the idea of my presenting one of the several, generally modern and comparatively little-known, concertos for percussion was as yet too innovative for their popular audiences. However, as a result of my increasing reputation as a musician, they were happy to offer me the opportunity for a recital, an extraordinary honour for any musician, and particularly outstanding for a percussionist who was still only 23 years old.

I was asked to submit the programme of works a good six months in advance, something I find difficult as my ideas about what pieces work well together change all the time. After a lot of deliberation, I selected six works that I thought would appeal to a broad audience that was bound to include a number of young children. I didn't want to put them off percussion for life by a battery of heavy works! Instead I aimed at a varied programme that would exhibit a number of instruments, so that the audience could appreciate what can be achieved by individual members of the percussion family. One of my favourite instruments is the marimba – an instrument similar to a xylophone but deeper and more resonant in tone – which was featured in four of the works and, as the BBC announcer commented, the enraptured faces of the little boys sitting in the front row suggested that it certainly won at least two fans that evening!

Apart from the Chopin, I selected Toshimitsu Tanaka's Two Movements for Marimba, an energetic and rhythmic piece, that exploits the technical possibilities and range of sound of this versatile instrument. Keiko Abe's *Michi* allows for improvisational interpretations, an opportunity to express my deepest feelings. I also selected a slightly longer and thrilling marimba work, Paul Creston's Concertina for Marimba, written in March 1940 at a time when America was discovering the possibilities of percussion, as Oriental, African and Latin American influences flooded in, and jazz was finding its distinctive and compelling voice.

Another America piece was Paul Price's exciting Exhibition Snare Drum Solo No 1, which is exactly what it says: a demonstration of snare drum techniques. It involves some spectacular effects: drum rolls, and notes played on the rim of the drum and on the sticks themselves, as well as fingerwork and the use of a handkerchief to mute the drum. Snare drum experts may admire the technical virtuosity, but for the lay listener – and viewer – the piece offers a continuous run of rhythmic and visual delights, and the audience enjoyed it as much as I did.

One of the problems before the Prom was finding the time for extensive practice, and I was glad to have chosen works that were a familiar part of my repertoire. However, I did decide to introduce a new and challenging composition: the Scottish composer John McLeod's *The Song of Dionysius*. This was the world premiere of the work, and it involved considerable concentration by both Philip and myself to master its technical and interpretative demands. John is very interested in the musical possibilities of percussion and had already composed a work especially for me, the Concerto for Percussion. *The Song of Dionysius* is a shorter piece based on the story of the Greek Dionysius the Elder, who was so suspicious about what people might be saying about him that he built a subterranean cave in the form of a human ear, with the acoustics designed so that he could clearly hear what was being said by the prisoners he kept in the chamber above the cave. The work experiments with sound and echoes, and begins with me playing the piano and Philip at the percussion instruments. As the piece progresses, we change places and take up our customary positions. The array of instruments required by John is always imposing; this time the cluster included tam-tams, tom-toms, temple blocks, cowbells, sizzle cymbals, Chinese cymbals, stones and claves, mark tree, bell tree, Japanese cup bells, marimba and piano.

Apart from planning the programme, I also spent time deciding what to wear. I wanted to look approachable rather than formal, so that the audience would feel that I was part of them rather than isolated in a world of my own. I think it is very important to get close to your audience; if they feel the performer is accessible then they will be more likely to relax and open themselves to the music. This is one of the reasons that I like to announce my programme myself, so that the audience have an immediate sense of who I am.

I decided to wear trousers in order to move as freely as possible, and found a pair in soft black material that were so very flared that they looked almost like a skirt. The Scottish designer Betty Davies made me a little fitted jacket in heavy white wool with big silver 'thistle' buttons. A pair of sparkly silver shoes to walk on and off the stage completed the outfit; once hidden behind the marimba, I like to pop off my high heels so I can be as quick and flexible as I like.

The performance exceeded our wildest dreams. The audience were warm and enthusiastic from the beginning; by the end of the recital they were on their feet, clapping ecstatically, cheering and shouting for more.

In the end I played three encores, the popular Maple Leaf Rag, a Bach chorale and a sparkling xylophone piece by George Hamilton Green that started them off afresh. Afterwards my dressing room was full of flowers and excited wellwishers. I particularly remember one woman, a Japanese lady who had seen Keiko Abe's name on the programme. The woman thought that Keiko, a world-class marimbist with whom I had studied, would be performing and had come to my dressing room before the show hoping to see her. She was so disappointed when I said Keiko wasn't there, but after I played she came rushing back with a charming bouquet of flowers, beaming all over her face. It was so funny and touching to see her pleasure.

Also in the crowd queueing up to kiss me or shake my hand was my friend Nigel Shipway, an excellent percussionist who was playing in *Cats* that evening. Apparently, at five minutes to 10, just before my recital was due to start, he began to feel odd and said to himself, 'Any minute now!', and as soon as his show finished he dashed to Kensington Town Hall, just catching the end of the recital on his van radio. He heard the applause and the encore pieces, and arrived with tears in his eyes. It was wonderful for me to have this kind of support, and to feel that I hadn't let my fellow percussionists down. It was important for all of us that the recital went well, and I was thrilled with the success of this significant performance.

Needless to say, over the next few days I anxiously scoured the newspapers for reviews in the music pages. I needn't have worried. Stephen Pettitt wrote an appreciative piece in *The Times*. He thought that my handling of the marimba demonstrated that I was a 'showman par excellence'; but the whole Prom confirmed my 'remarkable technique'. He spoke warmly of *The Song of Dionysius* as 'forcefully energetic music, both imaginative and idiomatic', and played with 'disarming brilliance'. The Tanaka 'gave Glennie the chance to show off a fabulous variety of tone-colour and dynamic as well as a formidable four-mallet technique.' David Cairns in *The Sunday Times* wrote 'Glennie is a phenomenal player', and Robert Maycock in *The Independent* wrote flatteringly of me if with reservations about the music that 'the recital's heady air had everything to do with the flair and character of its protagonist'.

From friends and colleagues in the music world, I received heartwarming letters of appreciation and affection. Graeme Humphrey who taught piano at the Royal Academy of Music and was an old friend as well as an inspiring teacher, wrote 'I was enthralled, moved, stimulated – so many reactions to your magnificent playing.' Tony Palmer, producer, director and filmmaker *extraordinaire*, who had recorded a performance by me of *Michi* for his film *The Children*, wrote, 'I want to thank you for the most wonderful Promenade Concert I have *ever* been to.' Ann and Ezra Rachlin, my first major sponsors who were like a second family to me, sent me an excited scribble by fax machine headed 'Midnight July 27': 'For us the sheer thrill of your musicianship and wonderful virtuosity was extra special for we were witnessing your dream come true! Long may you continue to open people's ears and minds to percussion.' John McLeod also wrote to congratulate me, delighted at this 'landmark' in my career, and feeling that *The Song of Dionysius* came off brilliantly.

A final, deeply felt accolade came from my dear friend, the percussionist James Blades, to whom I owe so much for his encouragement and dedication to the instruments and music we both love so well. 'Congratulations. Tremendous,' he wrote; '*You have made history.*' Reading his words I had a sense again of all the time that had passed since I first began to pick out simple tunes on the piano at home, all the days and weeks and months of practice, the people who had helped me on the way, and the negative voices that I had had to overcome when my deafness was first identified, and as my musical ambitions developed. James was thinking about the public world of music and musicians; but there was a private and perhaps equally remarkable history behind that extraordinary evening at Kensington Town Hall – the story of a little girl growing up on a farm in Scotland, determined against all the odds to make a life in music.

2

Family life

I was born in Aberdeen Maternity Hospital on 19 July 1965. I was not an easy baby to coax into the world, and my mother spent several days in the hospital anxiously waiting while I refused to make an appearance – an uncharacteristic reluctance to take the limelight, as my family like to point out – before I eventually arrived in my own good time. There was another reason why my arrival was a tremendous relief; at last my mother, Isobel Glennie, had given birth to a daughter. She had been hoping that my brother Colin, born three years previously, would be a girl, and with him and my brother Roger, now an active 4-year-old, she and my father felt that they had quite enough boys in the family. When the midwife confirmed the welcome news, 'It's a girl,' my parents were both over the moon with happiness.

But I was not a beautiful baby. My mother described me as 'the monkey' and, with my spiky black hair and big dark eyes, I could easily have been taken for a boy. Fortunately matters improved as I grew older! My name was the subject of great debate between my parents, and it was only on the steps of the registry office that they agreed to call me Evelyn Elizabeth Ann. My father was very close to his sister Evelyn; Elizabeth and Ann were family names both from the Glennies and my mother's side of the family, the Howies.

I was christened in our local parish church in the nearby village of Methlick, two miles from our farm.

20

The minister, the Reverend Craigie Hood, had a special way with babies and it is rumoured that none of the many children he baptized uttered so much as a whimper in his arms. He retired very recently, but there is no sign of his organist retiring. My mother has been playing the voluntaries, hymns and 'threefold Amen' at the weekly service since she was a young woman, and my father remembers that his first view of her was playing the organ at the nearby church at New Deer. He had to wait a few years before he finally married her, but 'Everything comes to he who waits,' he says with gentle humour.

My father, Herbert Arthur Glennie, grew up in the north east of Scotland, very near to our farm. He and his twin brother, who died at birth, were the youngest of a family of seven brothers and three sisters. Both his parents died before I was born, but I came to know my aunts and uncles well since the whole family, except for two brothers who emigrated, remained in the Grampian region. Although his father was a farm worker, this was not my father's first choice as a career; he would have liked to run his own business, perhaps a shop of some kind. Instead he left school at 14 and went to work on a nearby farm, and eventually was able to buy his own smallholding. By the time he met my mother, he had established a successful beef and arable farm.

I have often felt sad that my father wasn't able to achieve his early ambitions; he might well have pursued a rather different career if he had had the education and opportunities that we three children were offered. He quietly tells me that this is why he has always encouraged us to take advantage of any possibilities that came our way. 'Make the best of it – as long as it makes you happy,' is the motto. Excellent advice, which I frequently remember.

My father recently confessed to me that his secret dream as a child had been to be a musician, but there was no money for instruments or lessons. He has a very good musical ear, although he cannot read a note of music, and used to play the piano a little. When he was young, he led a dance band, which was perhaps a surprising activity for such a reserved man, but he gave it up when my brothers and I were born.

His treasured instrument is a very fine keyboard accordion which he used to play just once a year. Every Christmas Eve, while the rest of the family attended the midnight service in Methlick, I would stay at home and eagerly watch him haul the huge box to his chest and fasten the wide leather strap around his shoulders and back. The beautiful mother-of-pearl decorations above the keyboard gleamed in the firelight as he played the traditional Scottish songs and reels that were particular favourites with both of us. Apart from our piano, these yearly sessions with my father were the only times as a small child that I experienced an instrument at such close quarters.

I always wanted to play the accordion myself and Dad would eventually lift the huge bulk on to my lap; it buried me in the settee. After a brief experiment with painfully unrecognizable noises, I would beg him to release me as the box dug further and further into my tummy. Now the old accordion remains in its black, slightly tattered case on top of the wardrobe in my parents' bedroom. There are holes in its bellows, but I wish Dad would take it out and have a play. I'm glad he still has it; just looking at that old box keeps my memories of the early Christmas Eves with him glowing.

My mother, Isobel Mary, comes from a family of six children. Her family were also involved in farming, both in the Grampian region and in the Orkney Isles, and like my father she was brought up in Aberdeenshire. I was only 2 years old when her father died, but her mother and my Great-Aunt Jeannie lived together first in the nearby village of New Deer and then in Ellon until Grandma died in March 1987, and we were frequent visitors to their house when we were growing up.

My mother has always been a pretty woman, with dark brown hair, a lively expression, and a slim but strong body, very necessary for her life as farmer's wife and chief farm hand until Roger was old enough to help out.

One day I came across a packet of old black and white photographs which had been tucked away in a cubbyhole in the lobby at the farm, and found a picture of Mum with a lovely smile on her face and dressed in a wedding dress and white veil. But it wasn't my father she was marrying! I discovered with great surprise that she was first married when she was 22, to a clerk ten years her senior, whom she met by chance when he was on holiday in the area. After living in London for eighteen months, they returned to Aberdeenshire where her husband started work on a farm, but he was suddenly rushed into hospital for an operation for cancer. He seemed to be recovering well, but while he was still in hospital, my mother lost her wedding ring. She was very upset and immediately went out to buy another, but Grandma shook her head. 'You'll lose your husband next,' was all she said, and a few days later he died. They had only been married for two years and for a while, my mother said, it was as if the world had come to an end.

Although she had trained as a secretary, Mum now found work as a primary school teacher and spent her Sunday mornings playing the organ at the local church. She met my father about four years later at a wedding, when they were 'partnered' to sit together at the meal. At first she was cautious about her feelings for him, but he rapidly overcame her doubts and they were married eight months later in the congregational church in New Deer. Perhaps my father was worried she would escape him again if he didn't move quickly; he was 37 years old and it was high time to raise a family now that his farm was established. They have been married for thirty years and have had a busy, hardworking and happy life together, bringing up we three children and developing my father's farming business.

Where my mother is busy, active and a born organizer, my father is shy and quiet, but he gives a strong sense of the determination burning inside him. It is his nature to keep his feelings and passions to himself, and in a way Roger and I are similar. We'll work and work to achieve what we want, but we don't broadcast our plans. My brother Colin is more academic than any of us, but he is less committed to a particular direction. I have often thought that Colin's brains and my drive would be quite a formidable combination!

My brothers are very different in both looks and personality. Roger is neat and wiry with dark hair and eyes, and plenty of quiet energy. He is a born farmer, very practical and hardworking. Like me, he has always known exactly what he wanted to do and has gone ahead and done it. He was an easy child for my parents to bring up, with no childish tantrums or wild behaviour, but he has always been open to new ideas and is extremely enterprising. A few years ago he went to Australia to investigate the farming possibilities there – a wonderful experience that he won't ever forget. 'It's all so new there,' was how he described it; an enormous area which has still to be exploited, unlike Scotland where centuries of farming have taken their toll of the land. But Scotland is where he has decided to settle, for the time being at least, and, when my parents retired in 1989, Roger took over the farm. He also runs his own fresh snail business, Glenardo Escargot, producing snails for the menus of local hotels and restaurants.

There was no question of the boys taking over the farm together; they have always been like chalk and cheese. Where Roger is full of common sense, Colin is a dreamer. He is physically rather different from the Glennie males as well, with longish blonde hair and a beard – well, usually! We used to call him the black sheep of the family, but I think what we really meant was that he is a quite untypical farmer's son. He's not at all interested in outdoor activities; what he loves best is a bout of solitary reading. He has a vast collection of books and for as long as I can remember has spent every spare minute with his nose close to a page, or listening to the radio or his records. When I started piano lessons, this caused some conflict because the piano and his record player were in the same room. Percussion practice made even more disturbance and he still shudders at the sight of a snare drum. Our bedrooms were narrowly separated by a small corridor, and even with his head under the pillow, Colin says he could hear that solid and relentless 'Thud, thud, thud'.

He is a great conversationalist and I have often thought he should use his flair for language by becoming a writer or a journalist. We did spend a little time working on this book together, but he became too frustrated by what he called my 'non-natural' use of words. Despite my sisterly encouragement to move in the direction I thought would suit him best, he made up his own mind and went to work in the Department of Agriculture and Fisheries in Aberdeen after he had finished school. When Mum and Dad left the farm he bought a flat in town and enjoys being near the libraries and concerts, and within easy reach of his friends.

I've grown closer to my brothers since I left home. We all realize that, although we fought like cat and dog as children, we miss one another. We can have sensible conversations now, just sitting together in the living room and talking, whereas before it was always jokes and teasing. I suppose we've all grown up. I feel most aware of this in myself when I'm giving master classes or listening to young players and I suddenly think, golly, they're looking at me with such respect and it wasn't so long ago that I was feeling exactly as they do. It's rather pleasant to find that I can understand what they are going through.

Although it is difficult to see my parents as often as

I would like, I remain in close touch, and am delighted when my work takes me to the north-east so that I can visit them. My father still advises me on business matters, and they both take an active interest in my career. I can even have a good gossip with Mum by telephone, although it's rather one-sided! I tell her when I'm going to ring, dial the number and start talking, while she taps on the phone with a pencil to let me know that she's listening at the other end. Mum probably misses me more than anyone else in the family; it's not just the absence of music in the house, but also the lack of someone to share the 'girlie' things with, shopping and pottering about the house together. She's lived most of her life in a man's world, brought up on a farm and then marrying a farmer, doing so much of the work herself.

My family have always been very important to me, and their continued quiet affection has been an enormous support in my busy life as a professional musician. I have many happy memories, too, of my childhood on our farm Hillhead of Ardo.

3

Hillhead of Ardo

Living in a fume-polluted city as I do now, I find my mind often wanders back to my days on 'the ranch' as I used to call the farm. It was a wonderful place for children: fresh air and water, and an abundance of open space with the freedom to run about and shout as much as we liked, surrounded by the natural growth of tree and plant life.

The seasons there were absolutely true and distinct, not running into one another as they tend to do in cities. Spring was beautiful with snowdrops, crocuses and daffodils galore sprouting in the garden and behind the main henhouse, and the lambs scurrying playfully in the fields around us. Everything was sparkling new, and the house was always cleaned and polished from top to toe to match. Late summer was harvest time, with hot and dusty roads and empty outbuildings which echoed as we played ball, or rode in and out on our bicycles. The fields of cereals would be brilliantly coloured, and speckled here and there with livestock. Deep browns and bronzes in the leaves and ploughed fields meant autumn had arrived, and then winter would prove itself with frost and snow and powercuts, and the warm living glow of the fire indoors. I appreciated every variety of weather as each had its loveliness and its role to play in the yearly cycle of the farm.

Hillhead of Ardo is the name of our farm, known to the locals less grandly as 'Hillies'; Hillhead is our personal title and Ardo refers to the district. The farm is situated on the brow of a hill, hence hill head, with other farms and crofts spread out around us as far as the eye can see. The view is marvellous. However, being at the top of the hill means that we get the full force of good and bad weather conditions, sometimes almost blown away in a gale, or freezing or boiling as the season dictates. Snow can block our bumpy farm road in minutes and a snow plough is an essential piece of equipment for local farmers.

My parents moved here soon after Colin was born. They were anxious to find a farm where they could settle for a few years while their children were growing up, and Hillhead seemed just the place. In the end, they stayed almost twenty-five years. The farm was eighty-six acres when they bought it, but they later purchased an adjacent farm, another fifty-six acres of land, and also rented other fields. The house is a hundred years old and typical of many farmhouses in the area in both structure and appearance. Built of local grey stone with white harling, the main building has two floors, and there are a number of outbuildings for storing cereals and fodder, and to house the animals and poultry that we reared over the years.

The kitchen was the focal point for my brothers and myself, a good-sized room which was both warm and welcoming, and I remember playing Ludo and Monopoly or drawing with friends on the big red table while the grown ups were in the living room. The kitchen was the centre for another equally popular activity. Home cooking was one of the delights of my mother's farm housekeeping. We started the day with porridge and fresh cream from our cows, with a haliborange tablet slipped on to our spoons to keep colds away in winter. Suppertime would be eggs cooked in one of the many ways available, followed by my mother's oatcakes. On Sundays we took the opportunity for family meals as our schedules often meant that we ate in relays the rest of the week, and the ritual lunch of Scotch broth and silverside beef followed by a surprise dessert was always eagerly anticipated – and I'm afraid rather quickly gobbled. Somehow we were always hungry on the farm. In winter months we would often eat supper in the living room, huddling round the fire to keep warm from draughty doors, and watching *Black Beauty* on television while we ate our softboiled eggs.

We had two living rooms, one with a pleasant open fire, the other called simply 'the room'. This was the 'posh' room, kept for visitors, and we children were under strict orders to keep it neat and tidy. It was also used as a refuge in winter whenever strong winds blew down the living room chimney, belching smoke over anyone who had the bad luck to be sitting near the fire. Unfortunately the heater in 'the room' was rather ineffectual, and we would jostle and shove one another to secure the best position in front of it.

This eventually became the music room, where I would practise the piano, and Colin could listen to his records and play the trombone. 'The room' has a large cupboard which contained an unlikely combination of alcoholic drinks on the top shelf and music and hymn books lower down. Nobody in the family has much liking for spirits, so the bottles would sit there untouched all through the year, waiting for Hogmanay to get their share of attention. When I was 3, my Aunt Evelyn wrote my name on a raffle ticket and I won a bottle of port. 'Save it till you're 21,' she said, but it hasn't yet been opened. I am teetotal, so it may stay there forever, quietly maturing while it gathers dust.

Another favourite room for me was the sun porch which was later built on the ground floor, facing south and looking out over the garden and fields. It was lovely to sit there in summer, catching the hot sun, reading, and having a doze in the rare moments free from farmwork, school and all other activities that seemed to keep us in a state of constant flurry.

The three children used the two bedrooms upstairs,

both quite large rooms with sloping ceilings and views across the fields for many miles. At first we shared one room, with the two boys in a double bed and me in a single alongside, and the spare room was kept for friends and relatives who came to stay. Our bedroom was directly above my parents' room on the ground floor with the result that they could hear every sound we made. For one reason or another arguments and fights always developed between the two boys at bed-time, and there was invariably some kind of rumpus before the household settled down to sleep. I can confess now that I was often responsible for starting the trouble by 'taraneezing' (annoying or teasing) the boys, and then, at the height of the noise, I would gently back out of it all so that when Mum came storming upstairs with a slipper or rolled newspaper in her hand, ready to sort out whoever was shouting loudest, I would be huddled beneath the covers pretending to be asleep while Roger and Colin 'got it'. I still chuckle when I remember their hopeless pleading that I had started all the trouble, which Mum never believed. She certainly knows better now.

When I was 10, I moved into the spare room, which was a great treat. I loved having a place of my own for my clothes and other treasures, and a 'girlie' dressing table which I decorated with frills and pretty ornaments. The only disadvantage of sleeping alone, and something that still bothers me, is that I hate the dark. I always need a light on at night. Now, it's no problem as I can leave the kitchen or hall light on, and in hotels I always have the bathroom light showing through the half-open door; but when I was a child, it was not so easy to organize. I felt I had to have the lobby light on, but Dad of course would switch it off when he went to bed, and I would immediately wake up and lie with my eyes wide open in case there might just possibly be someone else in the room. My father had no idea how I felt about this and it never occurred to me to make a fuss to my parents.

The furniture on the farm was practical rather than decorative. My favourite pieces were the big old-fashioned sideboards that stood in the kitchen and living room, with drawers stuffed full of all kinds of oddments. I made a habit of exploring these drawers in case I could find anything useful, and I have to admit I'm still something of a hoarder. It gives me enormous pleasure to have a good rummage in files and boxes that have been undisturbed for some time, to remind myself of happy memories, or to have a good laugh at the nonsense I've been so carefully storing.

We all had our own special places to sit. Dad's chair was always in the most prominent place, at the head of the table, or the best angle to watch television; while Mum sat wherever was most useful, usually next to the cooker in the kitchen or near the door in the living room so she could easily pop out to get whatever was needed. I used to steal Dad's place sometimes and remember some real fun as he tickled me until I squirmed out of the way, or sat on me in his smelly farm dungarees. He's not a big man, but he soon got rid of me when he tried that tactic. Instead of being sandwiched between the boys on the settee, I preferred to sit on the floor or roll about on the pouffee, which ended up horribly misshapen: I still have a preference for sitting on the floor, which sometimes surprises people who don't know my habits.

To the south and east of the house we have a pleasantly fertile garden, consisting of a lawn with flower borders, and the vegetable patch, where we grew our 'tatties', fruit trees and bushes, and the greenhouse where Roger used to cultivate tomatoes and marrows. None of us has green fingers, but there was always enough interest to keep the garden looking reasonably tidy. Sometimes Colin and I would put up a tent in the centre of the lawn in warm weather, and sleep there through the summer nights, but I could only do this if I had him with me. Colin loved to lie inside the tent reading and had no anxieties about sleeping alone, and he and Roger would practise for cub and scout camps by living on the lawn for days at a time.

The farm buildings were built close to the house, very convenient when struggling through the snow to collect eggs or feed the 'beasts' as we called the cattle, but not so much fun on hot summer days when the odours of animals and poultry, fodder and other stores would drift gently across the yard to assault our sensitive noses as we dashed in from school to grab a slice of fresh-baked sponge to keep us going until supper.

For many years we kept one thousand hens in battery cages in a long narrow shed that is now known as the 'calfie' shed, as we keep the young calves in there, each in his individual pen with two pails for water and food. As soon as the calves are strong enough to make us fear for the safety of their pens, we move them to a bigger – and tougher – enclosure.

Years ago people used to live in the chaumer or bothy, a one-room building next to the calfie shed, which still has a blackened open fireplace and the original walls. Occasionally we would meet people whose relatives had once lived in the chaumer, when the land was owned by the nearby Haddo House estate and the buildings were rented out. Now it houses a cold store for the calves' food mix and the family's bicycles. We often used to play there when it was raining as there is plenty of room to spread out toys and make a mess.

The farm is mainly livestock and arable – barley, silage, grass, wheat and the stunning yellow oilseed rape, but for years we also kept two cows, who provided sufficient milk (and cream for our porridge) for the family. Mum used to make cheese and butter which became very popular in the neighbourhood, and I was always nibbling from the huge basin of salted curds, which tasted wonderful. The cows were milked in the stable, although we had no horses, and on the walls we can still just make out the faint traces of the names of the horses which were housed there long before we came to the farm. Another feature of the stable is our sheepdog Floss. We both go berserk with joy at greeting one another when I return home.

A favourite playground for Roger and myself was the tall grain tower, painted a splendidly glossy navy blue; only we two dared venture the thirty-five feet up to the top, but we loved to scale the slender ladder that runs up the side of the tower to gaze out over the rich earth and crop colours of the fields around. To the west we could view the braes of Gight and the hills leading to Cairnorrie, and in front of the vast woodland estate of Haddo House, the home of June Gordon, Lady Aberdeen, and the village of Methlick with its prominent church spire. Town-bred friends often ask me how we know which of the many fields are ours. 'Pick one with a good crop!' is my thrifty answer. One of our fields has a small quarry where we used to picnic in summer, and I remember running naked among the stones on the long hot days.

As I've suggested, smells are a noticeable feature of the farm, and the byre and what we call the court (which we pronounce coo-art), another large shed, are richly scented. We keep the mature livestock here, and the steamy smells of animals, straw, hay, silage and treacle can be quite overpowering. When I was small I had a tiny, light green wooden barrow which I used to fill with silage and sliced turnips to help Dad feed the cattle in the court. I wouldn't go anywhere without my barrow, and once we had finished our jobs and were ready to lock up, I would carefully store it away next to Dad's. The difference in size between the two always made us giggle.

There were numerous cats around the farm and they chose the court to give birth to their kittens among the bales of straw. There were so many that it was a problem to find homes for them all, but I so enjoyed rearing the kittens, watching over them in a straw-filled box until they were old enough to be given away.

I loved the farm and often think about my days as a farmer's daughter. When my schedule gets a little too busy and things start to pile up around me, I have only to close my eyes to see the dear familiar white house amidst those peaceful green fields, and the pressures melt away; I am a child again, idling in the sunshine or hanging off the top of the grain tower, craning my neck to see further and yet further into the blue distance above my head.

4

A very ordinary childhood

People are often astonished when I tell them that I had a very ordinary childhood. My life was like that of any other local child brought up on a farm, with lots of fresh air and outdoor activities, and the usual routine of school and homework, while fitting in as much fun as possible with my brothers and friends.

The farm was the centre of our lives and each year followed the same pattern of care for crops and animals. We never took holidays away from Hillhead and even on Christmas Day Mum and Dad had to break off whatever they were involved in to feed the beasts and attend to our poultry. When I was very little my only contribution to farm work was careering up and down the henhouse on my tiny blue and red tricycle, terrifying the hens, to my father's secret and rather wicked amusement. Later I took a more responsible attitude, collecting and sorting the eggs, and helping to feed the young calves. My favourite job was looking after the 'caddy' lambs which had been abandoned by their mothers. At one time we had a large flock of sheep, which meant that Dad and the boys were often up all through the wretchedly cold winter nights during the lambing season. The caddies were handed over to me for bottle feeding, and if I managed to rear them successfully I would get the money when they were sold. This was sometimes as much as £45, so was well worth the effort. They usually lived in the stable in a little pen stacked with straw, but if they were very weak we would keep them warm in the kitchen on an old rug. I used to get very attached to my wee charges, who obviously regarded me as 'mum' and, even when they were too old for bottle feeding, would follow me around the fields, bleating pathetically and making me feel terribly mean.

I loved all the farm creatures except the three geese. They lived on the courtyard and relished a good chase; as soon as they caught me they would push me over and nip my bottom hard, a terrifying experiencing for a toddler. Perhaps because I was surrounded by living playmates of all shapes and sizes, I had little interest in toys. I did have a small pink teddy bear who spent most of his time hanging by his ears from the washing line, as I was always pestering Mum to drop him in the suds on washing day. I also had a huge doll which I've still got somewhere, although she long ago lost all her hair; but I still preferred teddy bears to dolls, and cats were best of all, they were so warm and soft to cuddle. Aunt Evelyn gave me 'the doll' as I somewhat unimaginatively called it; she and Uncle Jim had no children of their own and used to spoil us with presents and treats. It was always fun to visit them, as she worked in a large house at Downside which had huge grounds and woodlands where we could run around and collect pine cones.

We took time off as a family whenever we could. We never went to the cinema or theatre, in fact my first visit to the cinema was when I went to Bristol for a percussion concert at the age of 16; our trips were very much confined to the community and districts near the farm. A favourite treat was to go for a 'run' – an evening drive in summer, exploring new roads and countryside, and stopping off for a 'chew', an ice-cream, in one of the little villages around Turriff. I always had to sit in the middle between the two boys, and remember the bother of where to put my legs as they grew too long to dangle over the hump of the brake box.

Less popular was the weekly visit to church, where Mum would install herself at the organ and the rest of us would sit on a hard wooden pew which we shared with an elderly couple. I was always positioned behind a pillar and could see very little of the proceedings; the pew was also extremely uncomfortable and I used to long for our neighbours to stay at home to give me an excuse to borrow their cushion and doze off in comfort.

My Sunday best was a burgundy velvet dress handed down by one of my many cousins. Nearly all my clothes were hand-me-downs when I was a little girl. I also had a grey coat with fur trims round the cuffs and collar, and a lovely warm hand muff where I used to keep a secret store of sweets to munch through the service. These 'dressed-up' clothes were only for special occasions. I usually wore trousers and dungarees, and was the despair of my mother because I would rarely consent to put on a skirt or dress. I felt happiest in clothes that allowed me to stretch and run and ride my bicycle. Even in winter, outdoor games were favourite with Roger and myself, playing snowballs and speeding down the hills on our flat wooden sledges, warmly wrapped in woolly scarves and jumpers and our colourful 'toorie' hats with a bobble on top.

Winter inevitably brought havoc, with loss of power, and no means of communication except by foot as all the roads were blocked. My father would clear a way with his snow plough, and shopping trips to the nearby village of Methlick would often be done by tractor. Dad would drive and Mum, the boys and I would bump along behind in the cart. I always had a store of snow-balls, and would lie low and then pop up to hurl them at unsuspecting passers-by. It always amused me to see Mum in the cart – our church organist trying to look dignified as she bounced along with a pack of unruly children.

The countryside was stunning in winter; the brilliant whiteness of the land glittered morning and night with the sun and the moon, and I often thought that it was a shame that people existed in the midst of this perfection, ploughing through it and making everything look haggard. Each year I used to build a family of snowmen under the kitchen window, ranging from tiny to as big as I could push, with carrot noses, stone eyes and straw hair, and dressed in Dad's old scarves and hats. At night, the light would stream out of the window, gleaming on their pale bodies and casting strange shadows across the snowy lawn. A less popular activity was the construction of a 'slidey', a treacherous patch of ice from the house door to the coal and tool sheds, so that everyone was forced to cross its shimmering surface at some time in the day.

We had to live through many long winter nights with no power. The only heat was from the glow of the fire, and we would play cards and dominoes by candlelight before shivering our way early to bed. By the time I was 12 years old, I couldn't hold conversations in the dark, and we would shine a torch on each person's face as they spoke so that I could lip-read. Colin still jokes about all the nasty things they were able to say about me, without my being able to hear. Sometimes the power cuts would last for days and Mum would be struggling to cook rather stodgy basic meals on a tiny gas cooker that took hours to heat up the food.

We had lots of visitors and, as a tiny child, I particularly loved it when Dad's friends called in. They would pick me up and whizz me through the air, or let me hobble round the room with my feet on their big boots. I liked to climb on their knees or ride piggyback, and was never afraid to make frank personal observations. 'Skin!' I would shout, discovering the inevitable bald patch at the back of their heads, and they would tickle me in punishment until I begged for mercy. I am grateful to those forthright farming folk for providing me with a ready fund of colourful swearwords which I happily rehearse when having a particularly bad practice session.

This was not the only form of learning that went on at home. Mum did her best to teach me simple forms of reading, writing and numbers from our farm 'library' before I went to school. One book in particular had a great effect on me; for some reason there was a book about wrestling in the cupboard and I was so intrigued by this that I became an avid fan of Saturday wrestling on television. We were all keen on television, and the first stop after school would be the kitchen for a piece of sponge or plate of cereal, followed by a pleasant hour or so watching children's programmes, anything from *Blue Peter* to *Scooby-Doo*.

I have no clear memories of my playschool days except that I always wanted to sweep the floor. Perhaps this was connected with my early ambition to be a hairdresser; Mum tells me that as soon as a visitor with long hair set foot in our house, I would rush for a hairbrush and happily spend hours pulling it through the victim's flowing locks. Later, after a trip to Orkney to visit some of my mother's family, I was so impressed by the traditional silver and black Orcadian jewellery that I decided to be a jeweller, making and selling my own designs.

I remember that trip to Orkney very well as, although I was 10, it was the first time that I had ever known my parents to be apart and I felt quite devastated at leaving Dad behind at Aberdeen airport. But it was also my first experience of flying, and the excitement of travelling in an aeroplane and visiting somewhere new quickly reconciled me to our separation from Dad. We stayed on the island of Hoy, the next biggest island to the Orkney mainland, in a wee cottage on the northern tip of the island next to the Old Man of Hoy. Sir Peter Maxwell Davies lives near there, and I was to meet him on a later trip to Orkney when I played in the St Magnus Cathedral at Kirkwall in the summer of 1982.

Mum and I travelled to and from the mainland in a tiny boat, and I so much enjoyed the scenery – the islands with their hills and bays and the sea very close on every side. We also caught a glimpse of the writer and poet George Mackay Brown, who has lived in Orkney since he was born there in 1921. Despite being so well known, he surprised me by what I then considered his rather down-and-out appearance; he would stand on the pier in his shabby old coat, and people said, 'Look, that's George Mackay Brown.'

It was a holiday to remember, just one of the many halcyon periods that I seem to recall when I look back on those days. It is so often said that we recall our childhood through golden spectacles, but I don't think that I have particularly embellished mine. We did have happy times, and being able to do exactly what I wanted during holiday periods was a freedom that I greatly treasured.

5

Halcyon days

The trip to Orkney was one of the few occasions when I left the farm before music offered the opportunity to travel during my teens, but our holidays were never dull. I hardly missed a day off school through illness. This meant that the holidays were all the more eagerly anticipated because of the prospect of a break from the routine of classes and playtimes, marked off for us by the clanging of the heavy school bell.

In summer the bumpy old road leading to the farm would be dry with heat, and I loved to heap up the dust in mounds in the middle of the road and ride through them at top speed, scattering a fine film all over the road, my bicycle and me. Some days we would set off on our bikes, with a picnic wrapped up in our saddle-bags, to visit Gight Castle. This is now in ruins, but was once a great fortification in the valley of the braes of Gight, overlooking the Ythan river. The castle belonged for a time to Lord Byron's mother, whose husband squandered her fortune and the estate was purchased in 1787 by the third Earl of Aberdeen for his son George, Lord Haddo. This unfortunate man was killed in a riding accident when his horse was startled by a young servant girl, and Lady Haddo and her family soon left the castle, which was allowed to fall into decay.

The long avenue leading to the castle from the main road is narrow and bumpy, and very dark because of the thick screen of trees on either side. The boys used to love to frighten me by pretending that they could see ghosts peering between the branches or human remains through the gaps between the trees. On one occasion I had to leave my friends at the castle in order to be home for a dental appointment. All I can say is that I made it along that path in double-quick time; Sebastian Coe couldn't have done better.

On the fringe of the castle grounds there is a whirl-pool called the Hagberry Pot. This too has a story attached to it. During the Civil War in the 1640s, the castle was threatened by the Covenanting Army so the laird, Sir George Gordon, wrapped up his silver plate and, weighting it with the iron castle gate, sank it in the Pot. The laird was arrested and executed in Edinburgh, but some time later a diver was sent to the bottom to recover the treasure. He reported that it was no longer there and that the Devil had taken it to his own dark kingdom. The diver was sent down again with instructions to find the treasure at his peril, and perilous indeed it proved to be. When his body was pushed out of the swirling waters, he was discovered to have been drowned and quartered, his grisly reward for attempting to pry into the realms of darkness. Whatever the truth of this story, legend has it that the Pot is bottomless and that if you were so unlucky as to fall in, you would be sucked down and down forever. There was a bridge that stretched across the Pot, but it was so flimsy and broken in parts that I never dared to cross it.

One time I found a desolate little wooden house, tucked away among the trees at the far end of the estate. Peering through the gloom of the filthy window, I was sure I saw blood on the floor . . . But Gight was also a place for fun and laughter; at Easter we would roll our painted eggs down the braes, and we children had games and adventures galore in the woods and fields around the ruins.

October was our month for accumulating riches –

but did we have to suffer for it! Yes, it was 'tattie' time. Scores of kids and a handful of adults would visit the local farmers to help them pick their fields of potatoes. I worked nearly every year, choosing the farmer who was paying most. My greatest earnings for one day's work (about ten hours) were £12; my worst were £5. I have what I consider to be an undeserved reputation for thrift among my family; my mother always says when she tells the story of how I swallowed a curtain ring at the age of 1, 'Well, Evelyn, seems you have held on to everything since.' Perhaps my potato-picking exploits encouraged this idea. The days were long and hard, and the weather was always appalling; rain, wind and gales to complete the miserable atmosphere. Every day was going to be my last, but somehow the thought of those pound notes at the end of it just kept me grubbing on. Every night I would store my money in a jam jar after counting it out carefully.

Colin always earned more than me because he was a 'sculler'; his job was to lift baskets, or 'sculls', of tatties into the cart to be driven back to the farm. I thought it unfair that he should be paid more than we pickers, who looked like half-shut knives by the end of the day, but having tried to lift a full basket myself I realized that the scullers were tough 'loons'. Roger earned the grandest amount of all – for driving the tractor, sitting cosy and warm, listening to the radio all day, and returning home without an ounce of mud on his wellies! He used to drive past grinning like a Cheshire cat, knowing that we were cold, wet and in pain. But it was worth it all when I came to spend my wages. I loved being able to splash out on clothes, or presents for the family, with money that I had earned entirely by myself.

Birthdays were never taken very seriously in our family, and these days I'm lucky to get so much as a card from one of my brothers. Christmas was much more of a celebration. Our house was always warm with a coal fire permanently burning, and cards would litter the living room, covering the walls, mantelpiece, shelves, tree and anywhere else we could pin or perch them. Everyone was nice to one another through the holiday, no fights or arguments with my brothers, and Mum would prepare steaming hot porridge and warm 'buttries', a special Scottish roll, with melted butter and marmalade to help us through the morning. On Christmas Eve, we would hang the longest socks we could find over the living room settee for Santa to fill, with a glass of milk and a square of Mum's homemade sponge and a log of shortbread to see him on his way. One Christmas, I saw Santa in his bright red coat with the white fur trimmings standing at the foot of my bed. Of course I closed my eyes at once and pretended to be asleep. Dad has always denied any knowledge of the event, and it's a mystery I'm quite happy to leave unsolved.

We used to attend morning service on Christmas Day, so all the presents under the tree had to wait until we got back – so frustrating for any child. However, we were allowed to empty our stockings, bulging with fruit and sweets and nuts, and one or two other presents before we went to church, and we would wake at 6 and dash in and out of Mum and Dad's bedroom to show them our treasures. No wonder they were always exhausted on Christmas morning.

For years we joined friends and relatives at Gowanwell Farm for an enormous Christmas lunch. Every course had all the trimmings imaginable and we competed over the lucky sixpence in the dumpling. This was followed by more presents and the Queen's Speech, before we trooped home to feed the livestock. In the evenings, we would gather again for mince pies, short-bread, sweets and Christmas cake, and a long and noisy card game called 'Oh Hell!'. I have forgotten now how this was played, but assume I must have known at least some of the rules as I was always requisitioned as referee and scorekeeper. Maybe that explains why so much of

right hand, which may explain the twangy noises that were all I was able to produce. Later my parents bought me a mouth organ from Bruce Miller's music shop in Aberdeen, but by this time I had begun to concentrate on the piano.

6

The three R's

'Fit did we learn? A' that we nott.
The Three R's, the bare beens,'
The School at Cairnorrie
Flora Garry

Shakespeare's famous schoolboy may have crept 'like snail unwillingly to school'; I showed no such reluctance on my first day at Cairnorrie Primary School, a small country school a mile and a half from our farm. My father had been a pupil there, so it was the natural choice for the junior Glennies. During my time, it was a two-teacher school, with about forty-three children aged between 5 and 12, housed in two classrooms in a pleasant greystone building with a yard and bicycle shed, and a playing field at the back. The head teacher lived in a house adjacent to the school building, and I remember Mrs Merrilees, who was head during my latter years at the school, complaining about the inadequate heating in winter. She was an attractive woman in her mid-twenties, who loved the school and took a genuine interest in her pupils. She was the first person to realize quite what a problem I was having with my hearing and to encourage my parents to seek professional advice. But this was still some time in the future when I was sent off in August 1970, washed and brushed by Mum until I gleamed, without a tear or a backward glance.

The pupils were divided into two groups, the 5- to

8-year-olds, and the 9 to 12s; each group was taught by one teacher, who separated us into smaller groups for different activities according to our ages and abilities. Looking back on it, the two women must have performed miracles of planning and organization to keep us all busy, but it seemed quite natural at the time, and I don't remember feeling bored or there being any discipline problems. The classrooms were divided by a partition which was opened for special occasions, such as the Christmas nativity play and parties, and I used to peep through the slits to see what Colin was up to in the second class.

Stretching across one wall of the junior class were the letters of the alphabet with colourful drawings: *a* for apple, *b* for bat, *c* for cat, *d* for door, and so on. There was a rack of Ladybird books in the 'reading corner' which I loved to browse through; another corner had bricks and wooden blocks and puzzles of every description, and there was a corner for plasticine, crayons and paints. All around the room were cupboards and trays of equipment, labelled in big letters, with the instructions, 'KEEP TIDY – OR ELSE!' Next to the big green door was a crate of twenty-five bottles of milk. At the morning break, or 'playtime' as we called it, we were each given a bottle with a straw poking through the silver top. If there were any bottles left over, then 'Hands up' for another; my hand always went up.

The second classroom was more grown-up; no more alphabet cards or blocks of bricks. There was a larger reading corner with thicker books, full of words rather than pictures. Everything was very tidy, and the desks were neatly arranged in twos and threes rather than clumped together. The headmistress when I first arrived was Miss Yule. She wore dark heavy-framed glasses, and had a voice that bellowed round the whole school when she was angry. She made allowances for no one, not even the younger pupils, and I was greatly relieved that she left before I moved up into the second class. Roger and Colin were not so fortunate. Another feature of the second class was the weighty school bell which lay beside the door. It had a powerful clang which echoed through the building and which I could feel in every part of my body. Later it was replaced with a modern electric bell – but by the time I left Cairnorrie School I could no longer hear it.

On my first day I was equipped with a brightly coloured new pencil and an animal-shaped rubber, all I needed to begin my education, but I soon began bringing home more and more books to show Mum so that I could make full use of the small leather satchel which I carried strapped to my back. My favourite activity was to take a huge sheet of spanking white paper and a pile of 'chubby stump' crayons and let my imagination run riot. The crayons smelt wonderful and were easier to control than pencils because I could grip them with my whole hand. I could have drawn and painted all day, and bombarded my mother with samples of my work. When I was still only 5, I won an art competition that involved several schools; I drew a picture of a lady in a garden, in a sea of flowers and colour, and one of my cousins later saw my picture exhibited in Aberdeen Art Gallery: an early claim to fame! When I have a spare moment, I often still like to sketch or paint for pleasure.

Our mornings always started with a song at the electric organ with our teacher Miss Flett. Everyone loved Miss Flett; she was warm and happy, but authoritative, and very nice to be near. She always wore delicious perfume and we adored having a lift home in her little red mini, because it smelt so good. Miss Flett was very tall with beautiful smooth white hands and long fingers that seemed to stretch the whole length of the organ keyboard. She would sit there working the buttons and knobs while I watched, too fascinated to sing. She played everything by ear and was able to adapt tunes to her own particular style, and I still remember her harmonies. She was the first strong musical influence in my life, and was kind enough to let me entertain the class with my rendering of Youngers Special Bitter.

After the singsong would come the horrid part of the morning – sums! Maybe if they had happened later in the day I would have understood them better; as it was, the figures would stare up at me out of the ugly pages with no feeling of warmth or imagination. My two best friends, Isabel (Issie) Gordon, and Edna (Eddie) Cadger, did their best to drum what were probably the simplest of quotations into my head, but I hated the whole mechanical business. Playtime followed at 10.45 and we were sent outside for games of Stuck-in-the-Mud, Hide-and-Seek, rounders or Stringyingins (String-the-Onions), or simply a good natter under a tree. We called the playing field 'the park', and there were also two concrete play areas where we would line up our desks outside if the weather was fine. Of course there was always a wind and our papers would swirl across the yard, but it was fun. The park had a number of large trees, which were great for Hide and Seek and secret meetings. On the other side of the park was a littered area of wasteland which we called 'Cheynes' land', as it belonged to a frail elderly couple who owned the tiny shop next door to the school.

Unfortunately for the Cheynes, they were not fond of children en masse, but were constantly pestered by us after school as we burst into their shop to explore the contents of their sweetie boxes. While the Cheynes hovered anxiously behind the counter, we would stock up on Football Chums, Fizzy Lizzies, gobstoppers and liquorice. My 10p pocket money would go on Polos for my swimming lessons (2p), crisps (5p) and a Milky Way (3p). I had another 10p a week to put into my savings bank account and would sometimes pop my sweetie money in there too, but very rarely, as I hated swimming trips without something to suck. Even today I carry what the Americans call 'lifesavers' (Polo mints) when I'm travelling to and from concerts.

If the weather was really bad, we were allowed to stay indoors and use the gym equipment at playtimes, but when my ears began to get more and more sore during my eighth year, I would ask to be allowed to spend most of my breaks inside to avoid having to go out into the wind and cold.

After playtime we would watch a schools television programme. My favourite was *The Thin Man*. It was so spooky! The Thin Man came from outer space; he looked like a piece of steel with a silver spacesuit and a blank face the colour of death, and he spoke a completely unintelligible language. I adored it and would be watching yet if the programme were still available.

English literature and reading preceded lunch, and gave me an opportunity to repay Issie and Eddie for their efforts over my sums. I loved writing stories; like art, they allowed me to let my imagination run riot. The world was mine and I could write about it just as I liked. However, the class star for stories was Suzie Allen, whose father had been world champion at tossing the caber. All the Allens had a gift with words, and Suzie wrote marvellous essays and poems, which greatly inspired me although I never felt I could match her natural ability. Suzie's brother Jay was my primary school boyfriend and we spent many hours playing together after school and at weekends in the Dutch barn at home. He was always keen to take me off to explore, and my mother remembers the occasion when he wanted me to go with him to Haddo House some miles away. I suppose the idea was that we would bike there on our tricycles.

'No,' said Mum, very firm.

'But my father knows Lady Aberdeen.'

'Well, Evelyn doesn't.'

We didn't go.

At lunchtime I would wave off Isabel, who had meals

at home, and go into the dining room for what was usually an excellent school lunch. At the head of each table sat the table captain whose job was to make sure that their members behaved and the table was kept tidy. The captain also dished out the custard for the pudding. Everyone loved the smooth hot sweet sauce, which came in pink, yellow or brown, and was served in glazed earthenware jugs. If the captain didn't like you, it was tough luck. Little or no custard for you! I eventually became captain of my table, and I think I was kind to my members. The serving lady's name was Dot, also known as the 'dinner wifie'. She was careful about food, and a stern 'Tut-tut' would greet the child who dared to scrape her unwanted dinner into the pale green scrap pail. I once put my foot in it by complaining to a friend about Dot's firm discipline. It turned out that Dot was her auntie. An early lesson in caution before I blurted out my thoughts too frankly!

The big 'break' followed lunch, when boys and girls would mix together for more or less rowdy games in the park and yard. There were four boys in my class, the two 'BS's, Brian Skinner and Brian Simpson, George Rennie ('Tablet') and Graham Gordon. Brian Skinner was known as 'Teeny' or 'Angel', both of which nicknames he detested. He was a redheaded freckly lad with the loudest voice in the playing field; the ringleader of the boys, *he* decided the rules of our games and that was that. The other Brian, 'Simple Simps', was quiet and gentler; he took each minute as it came, with the result that the simplest activity could consume hours of his time. He had a laugh like a tractor revving, which always left us doubled up with laughter and made him blush. His cheeks turned fiery red at the slightest provocation, and the girls would fan themselves elaborately as he went past, or offer to cook breakfast on his face.

My favourite games were netball, and football with the boys. Unfortunately this involved me in many a blow, and I remember rather ruefully complaining to

Mrs Merrilees that the boys had kicked me. 'Well, Evelyn,' she would say, in her quiet Scots way, 'if you choose to play with the boys, you must take the knocks the same as them.' Scant sympathy, nor did I deserve it.

In the afternoon, we would do 'projects', or sport, art, cooking, needlework or music. One term Isabel and I travelled the local farms taking photographs of hens for a farming project; of course, the hens would flutter away at the sight of these noisy girls with their cameras, and we would come away with dozens of shots of shed floors littered with hen food and droppings.

The journey to and from school was usually a leisurely affair. I would meet Edna and Suzie at the 'widdy', as we called it in the Doric, our local dialect, a clump of trees at the bottom of one of our fields. We would walk or bike to school along a back road where we used to practise our 'no hands' technique on our bicycles, or eat the gooseberries that grew along the dike. The road was full of holes which Dad and a neighbour would fill from time to time, but never with permanent success. I used to turn my handlebars down as if I were riding a racing bike, and this too required a certain amount of practice if I was to avoid falling flat on my nose in a pothole. Our neighbour Polly would often give us a sweetie if we called in on our way home, and we loved to pretend we hadn't yet had one. 'No, not me; you missed me. Honest!' We kept her and the rest of the community bubbling with our pranks, and eventually someone would mention the mischief to our parents; we would be held under tight control for a few days until everyone forgot and we could start our tricks again.

Almost all the local children spoke the Doric at home and to one another, and I still drop into it without thinking when I'm talking to my parents. The dialect is characteristic of the north-east of Scotland and similar to what is known as Lowland Scots, but it broadens the sounds a little further, and there are many terms and expressions that would be completely unrecognizable to a non-local. A fairly simple example of its everyday use was our frequent request to Mum, 'Are ye gyan doon tae the shoppie?' ('Are you going to the shops?') The Doric is a rich and expressive language, and it is a great pity that it is falling into disuse. It isn't taught in schools and is almost entirely an oral tradition, but it does have its own poetry, both traditional and contemporary, and the yearly poetry festival at school gave us a welcome opportunity to learn chunks of verse and recite them in front of an audience. One of my favourite poems is John C. Milne's 'Child Psychology':

> ''Twis, "Dae as yer bidden!"
> Fin I wis young,'

Sport was very important to me at primary school. I was proficient in most events and used to compete at the yearly Sports' Day. We were divided into house teams; my house Buchan won the trophy every year except once. Sprinting and high jump were my specialities and I also played in the rounders and basketball teams. I was even goalkeeper for the boys' football team for a while; maybe my complaints to Mrs Merrilees put a stop to that. On Thursdays we had swimming classes after lunch at Turriff pool. I loved swimming and won a number of awards, but I was only able to swim during school hours; there was never any time for my parents to drive me to the pool. Sport was a tremendous way of letting off steam, and I still swim as often as I can. Nothing beats exercise for relaxation and mental calm.

When I moved up into the second class, Mrs Merrilees became my teacher. Like Miss Flett, she was always a pleasure to look at with her fashionable clothes and fresh appearance. She was an excellent teacher and stern disciplinarian, and made us work hard. What made her special was that she encouraged each pupil to do his or her personal best. When she got angry, however, she really erupted; I once became involved in a noisy fight with one of the boys, and out came the leather belt, but by this time I was playing the piano seriously and I was spared a whipping to save my hands. Good fortune for me; my opponent didn't fare so well.

My days at Cairnorrie were happy, busy and productive, and it is a time that I look back on with affection and pleasure. It was a privilege to be able to learn my early lessons in that relatively peaceful and uncompetitive environment, just boys and girls from my own area, whose families were often known to my parents, and who were my playmates throughout my childhood. The lack of pressure on the syllabus meant that we were free to explore new ideas as they came up, and I benefited from having children of several age groups as classmates. At the same time, I was beginning to take a serious interest in music, an enthusiasm that the school encouraged, and my music classes and practice began to play a major part in my daily routine. When I rushed home at night with a bag full of books, as often as not it would be scales and harmony that were on my mind rather than the kings and queens of England, and by the time I was ready for secondary school, I had already completed six grades on the piano.

7

Tuning in

We had music lessons on Friday afternoons at Cairnorrie; our teacher, Miss Chapman, was a petite and dainty woman who always dressed in black. We used to sing, learn a little music notation and study the recorder. I quickly learnt to read music and as I improved on the piano, Isabel and I would be invited to play for the singing, which we both enjoyed. Mrs Merrilees remembers me sitting at the piano during breaktimes when it was too wet to go outside, playing whatever the other kids wanted. 'Play us a tune, Evie,' and my fingers would happily oblige. I played the recorder from 8 onwards, rapidly moving into the advanced group with Isabel and Edna; and I attended the Aberdeen music centre, Cults, on Saturdays to have more practice, competing successfully in the Aberdeen Festival of Music.

When I was 10, I longed to play the clarinet, which I had picked out when watching orchestras on television. It had a warm velvety sound which I loved and I was entranced by its slender and intricate appearance. A clarinet teacher, David Chandler, visited Methlick School every Monday to give lessons, and it was eventually decided that I could be absent from class for an hour in order to travel to Methlick to study with him. My parents made a secret trip to Aberdeen to purchase the clarinet recommended by David Chandler and I found it waiting for me one evening when I was sent to fetch the cutlery for the supper table, a beautiful shiny clarinet in a brand new black box. At first I had to practise with the mouthpiece alone, but was soon allowed to attach it to the instrument, and started to produce quite recognizable sounds. There was a finger-chart in the back of my clarinet musicbook and, unknown to Mr Chandler, I was soon busily exploring the chart so that I could try out my favourite pieces in the style of Acker Bilk. Our lessons went well and after a few months I was attending Cults on Saturdays to play the clarinet as well as the recorder.

All this time, I had been making steady progress on the piano. After my first attempts to play by ear the tunes and jingles that floated about the house from television and Colin's records, I had received the odd lesson from Mum and had gradually begun to work out what musical notation was all about. However, by the time I was 8, I was eager to learn more than my own tinkering could teach me, and Mum arranged for me to have lessons in Ellon from Miss Clark. Ellon was about nine miles away from the farm, so I used to attend the lessons every Thursday after school with Isabel, so that my mother and Isabel's could take it in turn to drive us there and back.

Miss Clark was a tall and strongly built woman in her 60s, who had the misfortune to be extremely short-sighted. Her house was old and enormous, with a vast garden surrounded by trees. At the bottom of the garden she kept two magnificent peacocks, and we loved to see them spread their tails to show off their brilliant feathers, stalking across the lawn with their crowns waving to and fro. We took it in turns to have lessons, and while one was playing the other would sneak outside and run like mad to the bottom of the garden to try to snatch a feather or two. The room where we waited was sombre, with big old-fashioned furniture in dark wood and heavy books placed neatly on the shelves. The soft tinkle of the piano would waft through from the room next door, the only sound to be heard in the deathly hush. Apart from chasing the peacocks, the one bright spot while we waited was the tray of tea and biscuits that Miss Clark would put out for us. Whoever had to wait first would enjoy seeing how many biscuits she could eat without the plate looking too empty. We both became extraordinarily skilful at this.

Every week followed the same routine of testing my pieces and my theory homework, with ear tests and sightreading as exam time approached. I quickly realized that, because of her bad eyesight and poor memory, Miss Clark would repeat the same tests week after week. I had very soon memorized every ear test in the book and could play the sightreading tests without a glance at the page, but Miss Clark was unaware of any deception and kept telling my mother how remarkably gifted I was. She was a kind and patient teacher, who never lost her temper or seemed to notice the tricks we played on her.

My homework was also routine: the inevitable scales, first the right hand, then the left, then both hands simultaneously; two short pieces, and an exercise or two. I enjoyed my home practice and made rapid progress. There was never any difficulty from Mum and Dad about my spending time at the piano, whatever the boys may have thought of it, and I was happy to sit for hours, working out any playing difficulties for myself rather than running to Mum for help. My father once said, 'Patience is a tremendous quality; seldom to be found in a woman, always in a man.' Certainly, he's the most patient person I have ever encountered, matched only by the great trombonist Don Lusher who I've worked with in recording sessions. Maybe some of Dad's patience has rubbed off on me; I certainly have no worries about working my way through knotty problems, untangling them at my own pace.

In June 1974 I was entered for my Trinity College of Music Grade One exam, and was tremendously excited about what was going to happen. Who was this mysterious person I was to play for? I didn't bother to warm up before the exam, and in fact have never practised prior to any of the exams or auditions that I've experienced since. I feel that there is greater spontaneity and freshness if I avoid the temptation for a last-minute rehearsal. The exam was held at Ellon Academy, and Mum drove me there in such good time that we had to sit and wait outside with a number of other anxiously early candidates. At the sight of their long worried faces I thought we had arrived at our dentist's waiting room; the only difference was the jolly-looking staves and treble clefs that adorned the walls as opposed to diagrams of rotten teeth and fillings. Mum was as nervous and uptight as anyone, remembering the tear-filled misery of her own preparation for music exams when she was a child. My calm only made her feel more upset.

The woman checking in the candidates was also in something of a state, continually assuring us that there was nothing to worry about, the examiner was *so* nice, and we must simply play our best, but up to tempo, please, as we were running late! After she had repeated this several times on a gently rising *crescendo*, everyone was shaking like leaves in a gale. I had no idea at that stage that the time would come when I would turn down my hearing aids to block out her fuss. In the meantime, concerned mums were straining through the barrage to catch the faint sounds of playing from the music room. Was that a false note or had the whole performance collapsed? Then the waiting-room door would open and in would sidle some poor youngster, looking twice as nervous as before at the sight of our staring eyes, or just downright relieved it was all over. 'How did you get on?' from all sides, as the music was hurriedly packed away in a neat little brown bag, and mother and child would beat a hasty retreat to talk it over in peace and quiet.

Now it was my turn. A cup of something hot and a plate of biscuits accompanied me in and were placed on a desk in front of the examiner. The room was long, bare and cold, with the piano at one end and the desk at the other. The examiner was small and elderly with white hair – and, unusually at that time, a woman. It was probably even more unusual to have a candidate who dictated which scales she wanted to play. I got away with it for the first two, but then she said gently, 'Why don't you try D major, right hand?' I got the message. I liked to look people straight in the eye (it's more often in the lower part of the face these days, for obvious reasons) which tended to give the feeling that I was totally committed to what was happening between me and the other person, and I felt very comfortable with this one-to-one relationship. With the examiner, it created a conversation between us rather than her just telling me to do this or that, and our time together ended with a bubbly 'Cheerio' and 'Thank you'. I went back to my seat with the proud feeling that I had met and dealt with someone new without anyone else being there, and for the first time had had a serious conversation solely about music. A week later I received the result. I had achieved Honours and the highest mark in the UK, which was encouraging news for all of us.

The immediate and very exciting effect was that I was invited to give a short performance at Aberdeen's Cowdray Hall, along with the other musicians who had gained diplomas and awards in their exams. This was the first musical milestone in my life and, to begin with, a rather daunting experience. The performers had to sit among the audience until it was their turn to go up to the stage to play or collect a prize. When it was time for me to go up, I didn't hear my name being called out and the man behind me had to tap me on the shoulder to take my cue. I finally climbed up on to the platform and was faced with an enormous grand piano with three pedals instead of the two I was used to. I didn't know which pedals to use. Everyone was looking at me and there I was on a platform for the first time in my life; I decided just to launch in and make the best of the experience. When the audience applauded, I had a terrific feeling of having all the attention on me. I liked being on that high stage, looking down on all the faces, and feeling a real sense of authority, and I suppose this was the beginning of it all, my thinking, 'Golly, I like this!'

Mrs Merrilees remembers that soon after this I said to her, 'I want to be a concert pianist.' 'So do a lot of other people.' Mrs Merrilees was always down to earth. 'But I have decided.' She didn't argue further.

For the next few years, I progressed smoothly through the grades, achieving six of the seven with honours and passing the necessary grades in theory to enable me to carry on with the Grade 8 exam. Theory was the one problem area when I first started to study music seriously. For some reason I found some aspects incredibly difficult to grasp. It was rather like maths where my mind went blank as I looked at the page of incomprehensible figures and diagrams, and Mum and I had many a tearful session while I struggled to come to grips with it all. Now, of course, I have no problem at all and can't understand what all the fuss was about.

I was also beginning to feel that my days with Miss Clark were numbered. We had our conflicts, particularly over my insistence on choosing contemporary compositions for the third piece in each of my music exams. She was wary of these and would never guide me through them, but I always received my highest mark for these pieces. It also began to be increasingly important to me to have a teacher who would work and challenge me hard, and eventually my mother arranged for me to study with Mrs Hunter, a gifted pianist who steered me through the dreaded Grade 8. Despite opposition from my parents and Mrs Hunter, I decided to try for this examination when I was 14 in order to have it out of the way before I started working for O-levels and Highers at school. I gained a Distinction.

But a rather more serious challenge had already had to be faced. By the time I was due to leave Cairnorrie Primary School, my hearing was so poor that my parents were advised to send me to the Aberdeen School for the Deaf. At the age of 12, I was looking at the prospect of being classified for life as disabled, and cut off from the music that was beginning to seem vital to my happiness.

8

'Percussion? You haven't got a hope!'

> 'The best that can be said about deafness is that it's an invisible handicap. It's not just the disfigurement of words and it's not just broken ears. It's most often a barrier between person and person.'
> *When the Mind Hears: A History of the Deaf*
> Harlan Lane

Going deaf was such a gradual process that it was many months before any of us realized that there was a serious problem. The first sign occurred when I was 8. I began to complain of sore ears after riding my bicycle in windy weather, and my mother eventually took me to our local GP Dr Gold, who gave me some drops which helped a little. Finally it reached the stage where I was spending playtimes and breaks indoors at school to avoid having to go outside. One day Mrs Merrilees asked me whether everything was all right because she had noticed that I needed to have words repeated rather often. I still didn't realize I was losing my hearing. My brothers were at the stage where they would make a habit of mumbling – you know what boys are like! – so it didn't surprise me that I couldn't always hear *them*.

All the pupils used to have regular hearing tests from an audiologist who came to the school. We all dreaded the session with her, not because of the tests but because of her attitude. She was so obviously bored with it all, and 'Oh well, here we go again' sort of approach which we found very dour. I had the impression that she rather disliked kids. We were fitted with earphones, and she would feed little bleeps through the phones and ask us to move coloured counters in response. If someone couldn't hear a bleep, she would say in a stern voice, 'Now come on, you can hear this; move the button,' which was very annoying. When it was my turn, I couldn't hear all the bleeps, and out would come, 'Oh, come on; you can hear this.' I used to get angry to the point of tears, thinking furiously, 'I'm not going to move a button if I don't hear anything.' Eventually she did make out a report to say my hearing was deteriorating, but it wasn't considered serious enough for any action to be taken.

Reading classes began to be a particular problem. I was in the top reading class with Isabel and Edna who were also quick readers; one person would read a passage, then another and so on. The teacher would say 'Isabel, Edna, Evelyn . . . ,' and I began to have to look up to see when it was my turn. Then my school results stopped improving, even though I was working just as hard. Finally I couldn't answer even simple questions in some of our test papers; I compared notes with Edna and Isabel and realized that I just didn't know about the subjects. I had no hope of getting the answers right. I began to feel increasingly bewildered. I didn't know whether the problem was because I wasn't hearing things properly or simply lacked ability, but I was ready to explode; I knew I had so much room to grow and develop, but I just wasn't getting anywhere.

By now Mrs Merrilees was very worried about me and told my parents, 'Evelyn's not progressing at all.' My family were also noticing a big difference. It all became rather crucial when I was 11, ready to move on to secondary school. My parents had taken me several times to Dr Gold, but he now sent me to Aberdeen to a hearing specialist. The consultant, Mr Wills, tested my hearing and told my mother, 'She needs to be fitted out with hearing aids immediately.' This was bad enough, but then he went on, 'You're going to have to send Evelyn to the Aberdeen School for the Deaf.' Mum was devastated. She simply hadn't realized how serious the problem was, as I had been coping with my difficulties with so little fuss. She told me later that she went numb at Mr Wills' advice, but I was undeterred. 'There should be no need for the deaf school,' I told him sharply. I had no intention of being sent anywhere where I would be cut off from music. Somehow I would cope with my deafness; it was just a matter of getting used to it.

Dad was waiting outside in the car, so we rushed to tell him what the consultant had advised. Luckily he shared my opinion on the matter: 'Och, let's not create problems. We'll let her go to Ellon Academy as planned, and if it doesn't work out then we can think of her going to a special school.' I was fitted out with the most powerful hearing aids available and, in the autumn, after passing the 11-plus, I went to Ellon Academy, our local secondary school, along with most of the other children from my class at Cairnorrie.

Despite all the tests, nobody knew quite why I had gone deaf. I had started to play the clarinet around that time and was keen to try all the high notes which I didn't yet have the skill to manage, so maybe that didn't help, and in fact my mother eventually stopped my lessons because she was so worried about my ears. I was also swimming every week, although I was less and less enthusiastic. If I had to do anything under water, I found it difficult to keep my eyes open and, with my eyes shut and no hearing, I was completely cut off. Maybe all those years as a water baby had affected my ears. The only explanation Mr Wills could find was that it was the result of some gradual damage to the nerves, but what caused it nobody knew. Later I went to have extensive tests in Glasgow which confirmed that I had become profoundly deaf.

My hearing aids caused quite a stir in our local area. It was unusual for anyone to have them, never mind an 11-year-old child, and all sorts of people from the postman to the chimney-sweep would stop me in the street to take a peep. They were the small variety that just fitted round my ear and were hidden under my hair, so people who didn't know I was deaf wouldn't notice at all. It took me a while to get used to the aids; I was able to control the volume, which could be turned up very loud indeed, and I was tickled pink at being able to hear all sorts of things that I hadn't previously been able to catch. But I also had the problem of picking up noises that didn't interest me at all. If a tractor or any sort of machinery was buzzing I would have to turn off the aids because it made such a din, even at the lowest volume.

My speaking voice grew higher and higher in pitch because, as sounds outside me got louder, I began to raise my voice to compensate. This sometimes embarrassed my family. We went on one occasion to a restaurant in Aberdeen and I was speaking so loudly that everyone turned round to look at me. Mum kept saying, 'Evelyn, don't shout so loud!' and I was protesting. 'I'm not, I'm not.' There was an old gentleman and his wife at the next table who seemed to understand the situation and they cheered me up by smiling at me. In fact I didn't feel particularly worried about these kinds of problems; it was more a question of learning how to adjust my pitch so that everyone didn't have to follow the thoughts of Evelyn!

The other difficulty was that the batteries were very tiny, rather like a watch battery, and would run out without warning. As I grew to depend on the aids more and more, this could get me into trouble. On one occasion, after I had started to perform music in public at Ellon Academy, the batteries went flat just before I was due to go on stage. I felt completely lost, all my self-confidence disappeared, and I said desperately to Colin. 'What am I going to do?' Luckily Mum was in the audience, so he rushed off to find her and she drove the nine miles to and from home in record time to deliver a spare set. It was a lesson that I should always carry spares with me.

Ellon Academy was quite a change from Cairnorrie Primary. Instead of the tiny classes and small population of Cairnorrie School, I found myself in a class of at least thirty children, and the school had a total of around 1,300 pupils. I was glad to be with old friends, especially Edna and Isabel, from my primary class.

I had decided not to tell any of the teachers at Ellon that I was deaf as I felt able to cope with the help of the aids. My first real challenge came with the music test. There was a strong music department at Ellon, with two full-time teachers, Mr Hamish Park, who was head of the department, and Miss Morag Shirran. Music was compulsory for the first year pupils and they used to give us an aural test to find out who was musical and who wasn't. We had to listen to a tape which asked questions and mark our answers on a sheet of paper. The questions were straightforward: 'Which is the highest note?', then there would be three notes and you had to write 1, 2 or 3. The problem was that I hadn't a clue what to write because I couldn't hear the tape. Either the tape or the equipment was terribly old and all I could hear was a horrible crackle! The music rooms were in an annexe, and I remember looking out of the window while this cacophony was going on and thinking, 'Well, it isn't important, it's only the teacher seeing who's musical or not.' I had already successfully passed six grades on the piano, which made me quite confident about my musical ability. My reaction was 'Why don't they get a decent tape?'

Having by now stored my clarinet away in its box, never to touch it again, I decided that I wanted to play percussion. There was a teacher who came once a week to give classes and I went to see Mr Park to ask if I could have a try. He was rather surprised and said, 'But look at your aural results.' He was too tactful to say it but I could see what he was thinking: 'Percussion? You haven't got a hope!' He obviously thought on the basis of the test that I was very unmusical indeed. I told him about my piano playing which surprised him even more, but he continued to be dubious until I pestered him so often over the next few days that he finally said I could talk to Ron Forbes, the percussion teacher.

People often ask me why I decided to take up percussion. It's difficult to say why exactly. I was quite sure that it was what I wanted to do, and my enthusiasm may have dated back to the time a little earlier when I went to a local talent show and saw a young girl playing the xylophone. She was brilliant, just amazing, and I thought, 'I didn't realize a xylophone could do this.' Once I went to Ellon I found there were many more percussion instruments to discover, which may be why I was so determined to try.

I remember going through to the percussion room. It was tiny, with one window, and what I saw was a three-octave xylophone, a couple of hand-tuned timpani (often known as kettle drums), a drum kit, an upright piano, books and papers stacked in precarious heaps, a great long cupboard for more papers, and bits of instruments everywhere; the room was so small and so crowded that I could hardly move. Mr Forbes told me to play some scales on the xylophone. You can usually tell when you test someone like this whether they have any natural ability simply by the way they handle the sticks. I'd never used sticks before but I picked them up and played with no stiffness or awkwardness. I felt just fine. Then he showed me how to tune the timpani and I tried a beat on the drum kit. It all went well until the aural, but he didn't seem too worried: 'Never mind, we can improve on that.' He went to see Mr Park to say we should get started at once and see how we got on.

Mr Park was even more puzzled; he thought, she can play the piano, there seems to be no problem with percussion, but her aural results show her to be the most unmusical person in the world. It was very strange. We have often laughed about this since. The problem for him was that he had no personal knowledge or musical experience of me; I was just one of dozens of new pupils who were tested by a routine method which was usually more or less infallible. Once he understood what I was up against he became tremendously support-ive and as keen as Ron Forbes to help me develop my abilities.

However, this was in the future; at this stage I still hadn't told anybody at the school that I was deaf, and my brothers and friends had also not mentioned it to the teachers. It was only when I had my hair cut some time afterwards that everyone saw the aids. The head-master, Mr Slater, was super about it; he just said, 'Evelyn, why didn't you tell us!' Everyone was so sur-prised. Some time later in my first year I was playing in the school concert band at a tiny nearby village called Tarves. There was a professional magician also taking part in the show, and during his act he wanted someone to come on stage to help him. He looked around the band and pointed at me, so up I went. Mr Slater was absolutely horrified; 'Oh no, not Evelyn,' he thought. Of course I coped fine.

I went on wearing my hearing aids until I left school, but they increasingly became a waste of time. As a musician I found that I was improving technically, but everything else was out of control. I was losing my balance and coordination, because sounds were extremely distorted and it was increasingly difficult to identify where they came from. When I was playing in a group I could only hear noise, and began to play louder and louder in order to hear myself, which meant that I couldn't relate to what my fellow musicians were doing. It was all very far removed from what I remembered as music, and I was so frustrated that I started to play with the volume turned down and then without using the aids at all. To my delight, not only was I no longer distracted by unidentifiable noise, I began to understand how to compensate for being deaf; I found I could control my movements so as to make soft or loud sounds, and I was beginning to recognize how much pressure I needed to strike a bar, and how the dynamics of a sound worked.

Fortunately nothing in life bothers me too much. I always think things will work out in the end, and so I didn't worry too much about what was happening to my hearing. I was gradually growing up, becoming more mature and independent, and I had the ability to concentrate fully on what interested me. When I was practising, my attention was on the music and trying to find all the ways possible to be able to play a piece and to hear it in any way I could. I never thought that I wouldn't be able to do this; I always started from the point where I was going to make an attempt to achieve what I wanted.

I was helped enormously by the fact that everyone was backing me. I didn't have to fight other people at all. The teachers would take care to speak directly to the class, rather than to the blackboard, which became increasingly important to me as I relied more and more on lip-reading. This again was a very gradual process which began as early as primary school. I found I was spontaneously looking at people a lot more, watching their mouths to see if I could make out what they were saying.

There were two programmes on Sunday mornings for people who wanted to lip-read, so I used to watch these and practise the lip movements in front of a mirror: 'Would you like a cup of t-ee-ee?' I think lip-reading is something you have a flair for or not; I happen to find it quite easy. As I became more fluent, I found it wasn't just a question of watching the mouth. When I'm doing the talking, I watch the other person's eyes to see how they are reacting, and when they talk I watch the whole face. If someone suddenly popped on a pair of sunglasses or a mask, I wouldn't be able to follow what they were saying; the eyes are so crucial. Once I stopped using the hearing aids, I became entirely dependent on what I could read from people's faces and general behaviour when they were talking to me.

I never learnt to sign, mainly because I was not at a special school and signing wouldn't have enabled me to communicate better. However, I do feel that a combination of signing and lip-reading works well for deaf and partially-hearing children.

Lip-reading is not much help with understanding music, of course. What I discovered early on at Ellon Academy was that I have perfect pitch; the fact that I can hear the precise pitch of a note in my head and place it exactly in relation to other notes has been a tremendous advantage. But music isn't just a question of sounds. To be a good musician, there must first of all be the seed that comes from the heart, something to grow from. I discovered that I had something inside me that had nothing to do with the technical side of music. Actually playing an instrument is a mechanical process which can be learnt from a book or a teacher. You don't only need ears to do it; it's mainly a question of practice. What differentiates one musician from another is how one understands the music and interprets what is behind the notes, putting one's own feeling into it, regulating the way the music moves. I didn't need to listen to music because I could read it like a book. I could look at a piece and pencil in my own interpretation, inserting the phrasing marks or certain words that meant something special to me, so that when I came to play it on the instrument I already had a strong feeling about the music that I was eager to express. This is how it has worked for me since I began to play, and all I need to know apart from the music and the instruments is something about the acoustics of the place where I am playing. If it's a studio, it's likely to be dry and flat, if it's a church, the sound will often reverberate against the high ceilings and wooden surroundings.

I did have problems tuning timpani. With pedal-tuning, you have a pedal that you raise or lower in order to tighten or slacken the skin, or head, to adjust the pitch up or down. With hand-tuned timpani, there are several taps at the top of the drum which you turn to tighten or release the skin. Because of my perfect pitch, I did at least know the notes I wanted to tune the drums to; and I discovered that, whichever drum I was working with, the slacker the skin the lower the note for that particular drum and vice-versa. With hand-tuning, I learnt how far I needed to turn the taps to get exactly the right tension for the note I wanted. Similarly with pedal-tuning, I learnt to identify the different notes by the way in which my stick fell on the skin. If it's a low note for the drum, the skin will be tight and the stick will bounce off immediately.

I can also tell the quality of a note by what I feel, I can sense musical sound through my feet and lower body, and also through my hands; and can identify the different notes as I press the pedal according to which part of my foot feels the vibrations and for how long, and by how I experience the vibrations in my body.

Ron Forbes taught me how to develop my sensory awareness. He used to get me to put my hands on the wall outside the music room and then he would play two notes on two drums and ask me, 'Okay, which is the higher note?' I'd tell him which I thought it was, and he'd ask me, 'How do you know?' So I'd tell him I could feel it maybe in the upper part of my hand, while I felt the other note all the way down to my wrist. Or we'd discuss what was happening in my feet and legs as I pedal-adjusted the skins on the drums, or listened to a piece of music. Similarly, I always knew when a door banged or the phone rang, and this ability to sense sound developed as I became more and more dependent on it.

Anyone can experience these effects, of course; it you put your hands on both sides of a piece of paper when the record player is on, you can feel the vibrations coming through the paper, and most young people have experienced the vibrations that pour through the lower limbs at the strong bass beats of a 'highpowered' disco.

I've seen these techniques used at concerts that catered for deaf people. I gave a performance in Brussels in June 1989 where the deaf were offered balloons to hold so they could feel the music through the vibrations. They were also sitting on wooden benches that had been rigged up for the sound to come through the benches so they could experience it through their bodies. Similarly, when I recently visited the Mary Hare School for the Deaf in Newbury, I was delighted to see that they had a huge library of tapes and the kids were walking around with Walkmans, enjoying whatever they could pick up, a mixture of sound and sensation, depending on how deaf the individual was.

As my deafness increased so did my involvement with music, and over the next few years I was to enjoy more and more frequently the curious experience of audience applause and recognition which I could see and feel, but could not hear.

9

Breaking the sound barrier

Soon after I became a pupil at Ellon Academy in August 1977, I began to keep a daily record of my activities. I have maintained this habit ever since, despite the temptation not to bother when life became too busy or demanding during my early years of practice, practice and yet more practice, as I worked to improve my piano playing and to master the exciting new range of instruments in the percussion family. Looking back at the diaries that cover my five years at secondary school, I am astonished to find how much time I did devote each day either to playing, composing or attending rehearsals for the groups and orchestras of which I quickly became an active and enthusiastic member.

Whilst I was at the Academy, there were a perhaps unusual number of musically gifted pupils, and this, combined with Mr Park's strong leadership, ensured that the school put on a stream of regular musical performances, including *Music for a Summer's Evening*, and *Music for Christmas*, and the twice-yearly shows in conjunction with the Drama Department, musicals such as *Guys and Dolls* and *My Fair Lady*, and the pantomimes *Cinderella, Babes in the Wood* and other traditional favourites. I very quickly became involved in these events, both as a performer on piano and percussion, and eventually as composer and assistant to the musical director (usually Hamish Park). I particularly remember some fun with *Aladdin*, which we staged at Christmas in 1980. I was by now an old hand in front of an audience and untroubled by the demands made on me by the run of performances, which always included matinees for the local senior citizens and primary schools as well as evening presentations for mums and dads and anyone else who was interested. On this particular occasion, we had given an afternoon show to the old folks; everything had gone extremely well and at the end a rather sweet old lady stood up to give us a vote of thanks. She spoke for some minutes and then seemed to stop, and thinking that she had completed her address I began to play on the piano one of the numbers from the show to keep the audience in a jolly mood as they filed out of the hall. Unfortunately, the spokeswoman had just been catching her breath for more congratulations, and my *fortissimo* rendering of 'You can make magic' drowned her kind remarks, to the hysteria of the cast and the Ellon Academy music department. No doubt on this occasion my hearing aids would have been found on top of the piano, which was increasingly their position when I was playing music, and my euphoria at the audience's enthusiasm may have prevented me from paying quite as much attention to the old lady's speech as I should have done.

By the time of my first *Music for a Summer's Evening* in June 1978, ten months after I had joined the Academy, I was a regular member of the school's percussion group and playing pieces such as Mozart's *Rondo alla Turca* arranged by Ron Forbes for the xylophone. These regular musical evenings offered a wonderful opportunity not only to play solo and group pieces in front of an audience, but also to have the experience of adapting pieces for percussion. The repertoire of music available to be played on percussion instruments has always been rather limited, and encouraged by Ron Forbes, who made many of his own arrangements, I began to explore the possibility of adapting pieces composed for piano or other 'main' instruments to play on tuned percussion. Exploring and developing in particular the solo percussion repertoire is now, of course, a crucial aspect of my work as a musician.

I also received my first serious encouragement at Ellon to develop my own compositions and had the excitement of hearing them played by other pupils, often at public performances. I remember feeling very proud when my Slow Air was played as a violin solo one year. Mr. Park was an enthusiastic composer and many a time he would say, 'Ah, Evelyn, I've composed a wee tune here; now what have you got to offer?' We had a marvellous rapport and rivalry which spurred me on to compose more, and I loved to be able to play my pieces for his comments.

My taste in music has always been very broad, from contemporary, jazz, Latin and folk to traditional Scottish songs, and at that time I already particularly enjoyed percussion pieces, or music that expressed a strong emotion or theme that I could readily relate to life – love or sorrow or the sound of rain. I had always found it fun to potter about on the piano, playing any phrases and tunes that came into my head, and even my earliest 'masterpieces' were rhythmic and percussive, and often scored for out-of-the-ordinary combinations, such as the cello with voices and organ.

My best Scottish piece was the Cairnorrie Rondo which suddenly came into my head as I was walking along the banks of the River Ythan, trying to compose a rather different type of piece. It was a good two-mile walk and by the time I arrived back home I had all the details complete in my head. When I tried it out on the piano, I realized that it worked just as it was, without needing any further thought. I have never been able to compose by sitting down and thinking about it, and up to now have always refused when people send me poems or ideas and ask me to write music for them. When the new Rector, Alan Cameron, joined Ellon in 1982, I composed a special Welcome which the school orchestra played for him, but again this was spontaneous and just appeared in my head one day.

I have never lost my enthusiasm for an audience. I have always wanted my work to be recognized and acknowledged, and what better way than having everyone's eyes on me? For this reason I particularly enjoyed playing solos, and realized very early that I was never going to be quite so happy playing percussion as part of an orchestra. Who would care or even notice that I struck the triangle in bar six, unless I came in at the wrong place? What I wanted was to have every note I played identified and enjoyed as coming from me. This spilled over into other areas; one of the reasons I gave up sport at secondary school, for instance, was because I felt swamped by being part of a group and didn't have the ability for individual achievement.

I did, of course, take full advantage of the opportunities to play in the various music groups at Ellon, the concert band and orchestra, the stage band and the recorder group. The concert band was mainly brass, woodwind and percussion, but the symphony orchestra included the full range of instruments, with a strong string section. Mr Park kept us busy with rehearsals; the concert band met every Wednesday lunch-time and the orchestra practised after school on Wednesday evenings. I became particularly frustrated by the orchestra meetings as I had to work extremely hard, counting the bars so I knew when to come in as I couldn't rely on my ears to tell me, but having very little real opportunity to play anything. The older players in the school tended to get the main percussion parts and I would spend hour after hour counting away to little effect. Colin was also in the orchestra and was very sympathetic, consoling me by pointing out that my turn would come one day.

Colin played the trombone, and the story of how he came to do this is as random as my interest in percussion and rather more bizarre. He was pottering along the corridor at school one day when Sandy Cuthill, the teacher who came in to give lessons on brass instruments, stopped him and said, 'You look like the type who could play a trombone'. He gave Colin a trombone mouthpiece to practise with for a week and then a really shabby looking old trombone. Colin took to it at once; he played with tremendous guts and enthusiasm, and really enjoyed the experience of playing with other musicians.

Mr Park became a great support, particularly once he had realized quite how bad my hearing was. On one occasion my hearing aid batteries went flat during a recorder group rehearsal and I was completely lost without them as at this stage I couldn't lip-read well enough to carry on a conversation. Colin often came to these sessions to help out, and Mr Park commented to him that he hadn't understood until that moment quite how serious the problem was. After that he couldn't have been more helpful. He treated all his pupils as individuals, encouraging each of us to work at our own pace, and during my first year at Ellon I made enormous progress in all aspects of music.

The other person who played a major role in my musical development was Ron Forbes. He had quite a background in percussion; after a spell with the Coldstream Guards, he had been a session player in London, before settling in the north as a peripatetic teacher, working in schools and music centres in the Grampian region. Every Monday he came into Ellon Academy to teach the percussion pupils. We usually had private lessons and I would miss one or other of my timetabled classes in order to work with Ron. I missed a different subject every week as far as possible, but the system still wasn't popular with the teachers. In my fourth year it was a particular problem as I always seemed to be missing Latin, a subject that I rather dreaded. The class consisted of only eight girls, all of whom I considered spectacularly better than I was, and

I used to plod along feeling like a real dumbwit. To my own – and possibly my teacher's – surprise and delight I still managed to pass O-level.

Ron's approach as a teacher was similar to Mr Park's. He encouraged me to play as wide a range of percussion instruments as the school could make available, and I was allowed to progress at my own pace, which was again very rapid. Outside the school, he ran a group of nine players from different schools in the region, who met once a week at the Cults Music Centre in Aberdeen, and I quickly became a member of this group. We were a variety of ages, between 12 and 17, and had different musical backgrounds, but the groups gave us the opportunity to play a vast range of percussion instruments, to develop techniques and explore new repertoire, and to enjoy both group and 'solo' work, depending on the pieces we played. Ron wrote and arranged most of our music himself, based on familiar Scottish tunes such as My Love She's But a Lassie Yet, arrangements of the classics, or pieces like the Autun Carillon which he wrote for our trip to the music festival in Autun in France. Although we didn't have access to the full range of percussion instruments – there are well over 600 separate items in the family – we played xylophones, marimbas, drums, timpani, vibraphones, glockenspiels, tubular bells, effects (such as tambourine, triangle, castanets and so on) and electric bongos, to name just a few. These produced an exciting variety of sounds from dramatic bangs and crashes to smooth and melodic harmonies. At first the group was called the Cults Percussion Ensemble because we rehearsed at Cults Academy; later, when we moved to the Belmont Music Centre in October 1980, it became the Grampian Schools Percussion Ensemble.

With the group I experienced my first taste of travel. For a year or so before I joined them early in 1978, Cults had attended the National Festival of Music for Youth, a three-day competitive festival held at the Fairfield Halls in Croydon each July. Around 2500 musicians from 80 schools all over the United Kingdom participated, with groups competing in a wide variety of musical classes, including bands, orchestras, ensembles of various types, jazz bands and so on. The festival and competition were all performed in front of the public, and it was quite a major musical event. The reward for winning one's class was the chance to play in the Schools Prom at the Albert Hall the following November. The trip to London twice a year became a regular feature of my teenage years, and my last performance at the Schools Prom in 1981 was to have unexpected consequences for my dreams of becoming a professional musician, but the first time I went to London as a rather shy and inexperienced 12-year-old all this lay ahead, and I remember being almost speechless with excitement throughout the coach trip south. I was the youngest of the group and, although they knew I was deaf and were very good about speaking directly to me so that I could lip-read, I felt rather intimidated by being with these sophisticated 16- and 17-year-olds all chattering away, and sat very quietly, gazing at the unfamiliar towns and countryside that we sped past on the motorways into the capital.

We stayed at the Key Hotel in Croydon for three days, so were able to look around a little as well as playing, but I gathered little impression of London and its suburbs except for a sense of the vastness of it all. I just couldn't work out how our coach driver could find his way around. It was a wonderfully exciting experience for me and the beginning of the love of discovering new places that has stayed with me ever since. These days I view the world as a great big village – everywhere is so accessible – and I just love to travel somewhere new and find out about the people and the country. The great joy of this visit was winning the ensemble category which ensured that we had a place at the November Prom, a success that we repeated for the next three years that I entered the festival with the group, and we all came home bubbling with enthusiasm and pride. Every year that we went to Croydon, our parents would come with us to see us off on the coach to London and would be waiting to hear the news when we got back. There were the usual jokes – long faces and a despondent, 'Well, we didn't make it this time,' – but then someone would giggle and there would be hugs and congratulations all round.

Playing in the Royal Albert Hall was a great experience. I was always overwhelmed by the sheer volume of people packed into the building – tier upon tier, so that when we climbed to the top of the hall to get an overview, the audience looked like tiny insects. I felt no anxiety when it was our turn to perform, just my by now familiar exhilaration at being in front of an audience, and a great urge to play to them and share my enjoyment of the music. The only worry as we climbed the ramp was whether anyone would trip over the hem of our floorlength kilts. The Cults Ensemble were dressed, as always, in white blouses with long pleated kilts in a variety of distinctive tartans, which always attracted audience interest. Although my family were Mackintoshes, I preferred the Dress Gordon, a green white and grey plaid.

Once I was on stage in front of this great throng I felt huge and powerful, and I remember my sticks flying as I played my heart out to them all. I was near enough to the people standing around us to have touched them if I had wanted to, and I could see all their reactions. We only played for six or seven minutes, a couple of pieces, and I just did not want to leave the platform.

The visits to London were my first taste of the wider world of music and I couldn't wait to expand my experiences. Luckily, Ron Forbes was equally keen that the Cults Ensemble should enjoy whatever opportunities there were to travel, and I soon found myself performing for appreciative audiences in Autun in France.

10

Striking talent

The Cults Percussion Ensemble were invited in 1979 to go to the music festival in Autun after one of the organizers had heard us play at Croydon. The festival took place during the school holidays in July so we were all delighted to have the opportunity for a trip abroad. Ron Forbes and another teacher accompanied us, and had the task of organizing eight lively girls (and one lone male) and an assortment of bulky instruments on and off ferries and buses, and keeping us in order once we tasted the delights of freedom from parental rules in the adult atmosphere of the festival.

We travelled by ferry from Hull to Rotterdam, which I found great fun. I had not been on such a big boat before and thoroughly enjoyed staying up late to 'bop' at the disco before going to bed in the tiny cabin which I shared with Miss McKinnon, the teacher who was assisting Ron Forbes. I was very bored by the scenery in Holland and Belgium, which was all very flat with not a windmill to be seen, but I loved France. Although the country we drove through was also quite level, it had the variety of colour and foliage that I associated with Scotland. Paris was a particular delight; we didn't stop there on the way out, but I at least caught a glimpse of the Eiffel Tower, and on our return journey had the dubious pleasure of staying overnight in one of the worst hotels I have ever encountered. It was old and dark as a dungeon, with a collapsing roof, but no doubt had been promoted to Ron as sensible and economic accommodation for his little team.

The festival itself was a great surprise. We had received little information in advance and were astonished to find ourselves the youngest group there among a crowd of adult musicians. We stayed at a hostel that also provided some shocks. On the second day, a crowd of Greek men moved into the adjacent dormitory area, which was only separated from us by a partition. This and the communal shower arrangements caused we modest Scots lassies some embarrassment, and I became adroit at extricating myself from close encounters with charming brown-eyed gentlemen eager for a little 'cultural exchange'.

Autun was a beautiful town surrounded by hills and fields of white cows, very different from the Aberdeen Angus I was accustomed to seeing. The weather was very hot, and the festival took place partly indoors, with concerts and performances at schools and halls and churches around the district, and partly outside, with groups of singers walking through the streets. We were well-received wherever we went, with tumultuous applause and the audiences insisting on repeated encores. It was all great fun. I particularly enjoyed the café life, staying up late to drink coffee or fruit juice and look at the local people. My spoken French was not very good, but I did my best to try it out, only to be perplexed when back would come a stream of words in reply, doubly incomprehensible because I was trying to lip-read.

The only blot on my pleasure was the beginning of some tension with the other members of the group, which continued to rumble below the surface long after the trip was over. None of the pieces we played were for solo performers, but there were main parts which were usually performed by the older members of the group. Always enthusiastic to master anything that appeared to offer a challenge, I took the opportunity of the free time we had in Autun to learn everyone else's parts while the rest of the group were out sunbathing or relaxing. This didn't worry Ron at all, he encouraged me to practise as much as I liked and it was a splendid opportunity to come to grips with instruments and pieces that were still relatively unfamiliar; but the other team members were furious with me, thinking that I was trying to steal their parts, and it caused bad feeling for some time afterwards. Fortunately I soon became a 'main' player myself, so was able to practise freely without being accused of 'poaching'.

The second trip to France the following year was potentially even more interesting, as we were scheduled to travel on from Autun to another festival at Vaison-la-Romaine near Avignon. This time, however, everything went wrong. We crossed the Channel by Hovercraft from Dover, which left me completely deaf, and by the time we reached Autun, a day late because our coach broke down en route, my ears were very sore indeed. The pouring rain that accompanied us all the way south didn't help. The interpreter who had travelled with us, Mrs Bain, insisted on taking me to the doctor when my usually robust appetite had failed for the third day running. Although I was always reluctant to admit to sickness, I was in such pain that I was only too pleased to try all the numerous and multicoloured tablets and pills that the French doctor prescribed for me. It emerged that I had an abscess in one of my ears, which was so painful that I could hardly bear any noise and certainly not the resonances of percussion. I stayed in bed. By this time my tummy was also causing me intense pain and Mrs Bain took me back to the doctor who diagnosed appendicitis. After much pleading on my part, I was allowed to continue the tour and spent a miserable night with a French family in Grenoble before reaching Vaison-la-Romaine. We had been away for ten days and I hadn't enjoyed a single painfree moment.

Finally I gave up. Yet another doctor was consulted

and I was taken to a rather unappetizing hospital before being put on a plane back to London. Within twenty-four hours of reaching Aberdeen – and a brief spell in hospital – my ears and tummy settled down, and I spent the next week regretting what I was missing in France. The doctors had decided not to remove my appendix after all, and I was heartbroken both at missing the opportunity to play in front of appreciative audiences, and the novelty and freedom of being in Europe instead of on the all-too-familiar farm.

Another big yearly event was the Aberdeen and North-East Music Festival, which took place in various halls and centres in Aberdeen in June. In my first year at Ellon, I played percussion with the Ellon Academy Orchestra which won the challenge shield jointly with Inverurie Senior Orchestra. I felt we had played better than Inverurie and was indignant to be awarded equal marks, but after the judging we had the challenge of playing one another's pieces just to see how well we could do it. 'Very creditable' was the adjudicator's verdict. One of my friends from Cults was a girl nicknamed Shuggly on account of the famous occasion when she managed to knock over a whole row of precariously balanced music stands ('shuggly' is a local word meaning 'shaky' or 'rickety'). In this exchange, she had to play my percussion part and I hers, which we both thought marvellously funny for some reason. I continued to compete and win awards in various events in the Festival during my five years at Ellon Academy, both in the school groups and in solo recorder and piano events.

Towards the end of 1978, when I was 13, I auditioned successfully for the Grampian Region Schools Orchestra. This meant that the following summer I attended a week's residential course at the Mackie Academy in Stonehaven, south of Aberdeen, to rehearse for a concert at the Music Hall in Aberdeen at the end of the course. The artistic director of the Scottish

Chamber Orchestra, Roderick Brydon, conducted the performance and was with us through our week at Stonehaven, rehearsing and giving advice. The orchestra consisted of around a hundred young musicians selected by audition from schools in the area, and the musical directors had their work cut out to mould the group together in the short time available. The works performed made no concessions to the youth and inexperience of the group, and I remember the following year playing pieces such as Mendelssohn's Scottish Symphony and Kodály's Háry János Suite.

One year Timothy Raynish, who teaches at the Royal Northern College of Music in Manchester, took over as conductor. He had already warned us that he was likely to get into a rage if things didn't run smoothly, and at one rehearsal everybody was a bit restless and noisy and failing to respond to him. All of a sudden, he snapped his baton in two in front of us all and stalked off the podium. We waited and waited, nobody daring to say a word or move, until finally he sauntered back, as calm as could be, and went on with the rehearsal.

The local press took a keen interest in the musical activities of the schools and young people in the area, and I began to keep a scrapbook of cuttings and photographs – the start of my brilliant career, I used to joke to my family, who were quick to squash any signs of big-headedness. My parents in fact continued to be extremely supportive both of my music and of my attempts to cope with my increasing deafness whilst at Ellon.

Percussion instruments tend to be expensive and for some time I would practise my stickwork for the snare drum on a practice pad. One Christmas, however, I asked for a snare drum of my own so that I could practise properly at home. I remember being tremendously excited as it became clear that my parents intended to take up the hint. One day we went into

Aberdeen to the main music shop, Bruce Miller's, and they made me stand at a distance while they organized something over the counter. Out came a big snare drum and into a box, but the business wasn't finished and I was quite over the moon. Could they be buying me a xylophone as well? I was having glorious visions of the substantial instrument we had at school, when a tiny glockenspiel appeared and that too was packed into the box. So much for my big ambitions! I swallowed my disappointment and managed to put on a good show on Christmas Day, and in fact the snare drum was marvellous and I still use it when I'm at my parents' home.

One of the reasons why my parents were so supportive was, I think, my sheer enthusiasm both for the piano and for my percussion development. They never had to tell me to practise, and my mother later confessed that once I had left home they desperately missed the sounds of music that had so constantly filled the house. However, I don't think any of us were aware of my impact on the outside world until my first big piece of publicity, an article in the *People's Journal* in October 1981, when I was 16.

This feature epitomizes both the good and bad aspects of publicity as far as I am concerned. Its four columns outlined my musical career and awards, and other achievements, including the Parker Trophy awarded by Ellon Academy for 'the most outstanding contribution to the school' in 1980. It also mentioned my ambition to go to music college in London, and talked about some fun I had had earlier in the year raising money to buy a phonic ear for another deaf child at Ellon. This was all very pleasant, but the headline to the article now makes me squirm: 'AMAZING EVELYN Deaf – but she makes music!'

I have always wanted my musical ability to be judged on its own merits, and have fallen over backwards to avoid favourable comment because of my deafness. I

take care that it is never mentioned on concert programmes for my performances, and have always tried
not to make any kind of issue of it both in my professional and personal life. Consequently, the news
reports that began to burgeon around this time, as I
successfully progressed towards training as a professional musician, now cause me as much pain as pleasure. At the time I was simply delighted to be in the
news and we would all excitedly read the articles, enjoying the fun of having the Glennie name in print. But
looking back on it, I do have reservations. The only
good thing about it, I sometimes think rather despon-
dently, was that the news of my success might have
encouraged other deaf and handicapped people. This
does in fact appear to have been the case, judging by
the letters I continue to receive from all kinds of people
as a result of my concerts, and radio and television
appearances.

I do have a fellow feeling for the handicapped and
one of the pleasures of my final terms at Ellon was
teaching the piano to an 8-year-old boy who had spina
bifida. Bobby was an outstanding child, brave and lively
and full of humour, and he made remarkable progress
with his music. He was a little devil, full of tricks and
games, and just super-alive, and I was very sorry when
our lessons had to come to an end.

During this time, my hearing continued to deterio-
rate, and there was a period at Ellon when I became
quite exhausted by the effort to keep concentrating,
trying to make sense of the diminishing world of sounds
around me. At first I was still struggling to hear in the
normal way instead of exploring new ways of listening,
and I became increasingly tired and bad-tempered with
the frustration, in particular, of not being able to hear
the emotion and meaning in the music with which I
surrounded myself every day. I always tried to keep a
brave face on things – the Glennies don't whinge! – but
one night even Mum noticed how down I was, and I

just snapped back, 'Wouldn't you be if you were struggling to hear all day?' She was terribly upset as she had had no idea how difficult it all was for me.

Matters did, nevertheless, improve. My diary for 19 October 1979, records simply, 'Really feeling another way to hear music', and with the help and encouragement of my music teachers, I did learn to develop other methods of experiencing sound. By August 1980, when I was 15, I was seriously thinking of becoming a professional musician, even though a visit that October to Mr Wills confirmed that my aural reception was deteriorating rapidly. A historic meeting only nine days later, however, cheered me enormously and was the first in a series of small and apparently unconnected incidents that finally led to my going to London to study at the Royal Academy of Music.

11

'A cry from the heart'

'There can be no happiness if the things we believe in are different from the things we do.'

Dame Freya Stark

James Blades is one of the world's great percussionists. Born in 1901, his extraordinary career has encompassed such diverse experiences as playing the drums for a circus band, and producing special musical effects for Charlie Chaplin and Laurence Olivier. He has worked with some of the outstanding composers of the twentieth century, including Igor Stravinsky and Benjamin Britten, and is a formidable scholar and beguiling lecturer as well as a performer with remarkable communication on a wide range of percussion instruments.

We met, perhaps appropriately, on Guy Fawkes' Day in 1980; our subsequent encounters have certainly produced some fireworks! When I met James, he was already an old man, a tiny figure in an immaculate dark suit, but crackling with energy and eagerness to share his enthusiasm for music. Despite being almost 80 years old, he was still travelling round the country giving lectures on percussion to schools and the public, and happened to be giving a master class at the Belmont Music Centre in Aberdeen. Ron Forbes took the opportunity to introduce me to James, and we played a timpani duet together, a piece called Circles on the marimba, and a snare drum duet. We got on like a house on fire and when we had finished playing, he nudged me in the ribs in his friendly way and said, 'You ought to think about going to London.' I was rather surprised because although I had begun to feel music should be part of my adult life, I hadn't had any practical thoughts about how to achieve this. I went home that night feeling very excited about meeting this extraordinary man and hearing him play, and his words had an enormous influence on me.

My schoolwork was beginning to play an increasingly important role in my life at this time. I was due to take O-levels in seven subjects in the summer of 1981, with three Highers, Music, English and French, the following year. Although I had made no definite plans for my future, I was determined to do well to make sure that I could secure a place on a degree course if I decided that this was what I wanted. My method of working has always been to move slowly and steadily forward rather than a last-minute panic to cram everything in, but I did begin to feel concerned that in subjects such as History which involved a lot of discussion in class I might be missing some important details. I was increasingly confident as a lip-reader, but even so I felt the need to do a lot of extra reading at home to make sure that I had really covered the subject properly. This put an additional strain on me and I decided to ask the school whether I could have some tuition from a peripatetic teacher for the deaf, Sandra Buchan, who regularly visited the school.

There was another deaf child in the school at the time, Michael Aiken, whom Sandra also helped. Michael had particular problems as he found lip-reading difficult, but the school was eventually able to buy a phonic ear for him as a result of my piano marathon. I played for eight hours non-stop, which to my great delight raised over £300. Unfortunately the ear made no difference at all to me, but Michael found it a great help.

My time with Sandra was very valuable. We met once a week for most of the year preceding my O-levels, and we would go over the subjects together, sorting out any problem areas and checking that I 'knew my stuff'. Sandra was very helpful to me in other ways; I found that I could talk to her about all kinds of things that were outside the school curriculum, and her broad and open approach to life helped me to develop and mature.

But my debt to Sandra goes deeper than this. Deceptively tiny, she is a powerful and determined woman, and her belief in me and her practical support created an opportunity that was to prove crucial. By the autumn of 1981, I had successfully completed my O-levels and was working towards my Highers. Around this time we had a number of careers advisers visiting the school and I had mentioned to one of them my interest in becoming a professional musician. The response was immediate and daunting. I didn't have a hope, and a number of mundane alternatives were offered. I was so shocked by this unimaginative approach and the insensitive way in which it was expressed that I didn't even feel upset. My dander was up and I thought, 'Well, I'll show you!' I went storming off to tell Sandra.

She took immediate action. She had been very impressed by a television programme showing a musical performance by pupils from the Mary Hare School for the Deaf in Newbury. The children were playing as an ensemble, impressively and happily harmonizing together with recorders, keyboards, percussion and guitars. On the programme Sandra had also seen Ann Rachlin, the Founder of The Beethoven Fund for Deaf Children, and had heard for the first time about the work of this charity. She wrote to the Mary Hare School to find out where to contact Ann, and sent her an impassioned letter.

Miss Ann Rachlin,   2nd September, 1981.
2 Queen's Mead,
St. John's Wood Park,
LONDON. N.W. 8

Dear Miss Rachlin,

This is a cry from the heart, in the hope you will be able to offer some advice. I have a pupil in Ellon Academy (17 miles from Aberdeen) who is an extremely talented musician. She is now in the 5th form and one of her 'O' levels was an 'A' – Band 1 in music. Her one ambition is to play in an orchestra, but, as you will see from her audiogram, those involved in her care are concerned as to the feasibility of such a plan. With your contacts amongst professional musicians, I wondered if you could offer any insight into the possibility of a child with such a hearing loss being acceptable in a major orchestra.

Evelyn simply lives for her music. In fact she has just accepted her first music pupil. She is a member of the Cults Percussion Ensemble which won their section in the Music for Youth competition in Croydon in July. As a result, she is returning to London on 25th November to play with the group in the Albert Hall. Also, this summer, she was chosen to play in the Scottish National Youth Orchestra and in the International Youth Music Festival in Aberdeen she joined in the International Youth Orchestra. I also must add that she plays with the Grampian Schools Orchestra. However, I hope I've given you some idea of the extent of her involvement in music.

Although Evelyn's hearing loss is so marked, her speech is excellent, but of course she relies heavily on lipreading. No one can understand why her musical performance, under these circumstances, is so exceptional.

I know nothing of music, but I have been told that, for a child to be accepted into an orchestra, may depend on contacts. So really what I am asking is –

would anyone in your acquaintance be interested in such a child? Within the deaf world do you know of anyone involved in promoting the cause of hearing-handicapped musicians?

I hope you will forgive such a long, rambling letter, but I am desperately trying to do all I can for this extremely charming pupil.

Yours sincerely,

SANDRA BUCHAN
Peripatetic Teacher of the Deaf

P.S. Remembering having seen you on television with some handicapped musicians, I wrote to Mr. K. Pearce of the Mary Hare Grammar School.

Ann's response was kind and positive; after talking to Sandra, she suggested that the best idea was for me to visit London to play for her husband, Ezra Rachlin, who had been a child prodigy pianist and was now a well-known conductor. It was arranged that I would visit Ann with Sandra Buchan when I went to London for the Schools Prom in November.

The Beethoven Fund for Deaf Children was the brain-child of Ann Rachlin and grew out of her 'Fun with Music' concerts for children. A professional storyteller, Ann has worked for many years to introduce children to classical music by integrating and illustrating stories with the work of great composers. She began to combine her concerts with fundraising for the National Deaf Children's Society, and eventually inaugurated the Beethoven Fund in 1976. The aim of the charity is to provide musical speech therapy for deaf or partially-hearing children through the use of special musical instruments. These are specifically designed to help the children to reproduce the rhythm and melody of speech and in this way to develop their powers of communication. As well as raising money to supply these special – and expensive – instruments to interested schools and units for deaf children, the Fund sponsors workshops and training sessions for teachers in how to use the instruments and develop the listening and speaking skills of the deaf. Ann passionately believes in the importance of music to deaf people, and the Fund has helped to revolutionize attitudes both to what deaf people are capable of achieving and to how they may be able to hear. My own experience indicates that there are many more ways than one of identifying musical sounds.

The Fund's supporters include musicians and performers such as the conductor Lorin Maazel, who generously and magnificently held a fiftieth birthday concert at the Festival Hall to raise money for the fund. Since then it has gone from strength to strength. Famous and brilliant musicians such as André Previn, Claudio Abbado and Sir Georg Solti, and the actors Sir Alec Guinness and Peter Ustinov have performed on behalf of the Fund, and Prince Edward narrated Prokofiev's *Peter and the Wolf* at the 1987 Christmas Concert, with the London Symphony Orchestra conducted by Ezra.

Glorious company to be among, and my later association with the Fund has given me the opportunity to make my own modest contribution to its fundraising activities. At the time I knew almost nothing about it and was principally concerned with juggling the various balls of schoolwork, practice and preparing for yet another performance with Cults, now known as the Grampian Schools Percussion Ensemble, at the Schools Prom.

Sandra and I arrived at the Rachlins' house in St John's Wood in North London on a rather cold and dreary day in late November. Ezra later told me that they had no idea what to expect; they had felt intrigued by Sandra's letter, but also rather pessimistic. At this stage, nobody was even considering the possibility of my becoming a solo performer. The only option apparently available was to play in an orchestra, and their one thought, as with everyone else at that time, was 'How will she manage?' What conductor was going to be prepared to put in the extra time they feared would be needed to guide a deaf percussionist through her part? Given the minor role percussion plays in many orchestral pieces, this seemed a hopeless venture. When we reached the house, Ann and Sandra chatted downstairs while I went up to play for Ezra on the piano, although Ann apparently crept up to listen through the door. I played Schubert's *Impromptu* in G flat. When I had finished, Ezra was obviously astonished and pleased, but although he was complimentary, he had to admit he wasn't convinced that I was up to being a concert pianist. This didn't upset my composure. Patiently I explained: 'This is not my good instrument; I'm much better on percussion.' Ezra's reaction was: 'She's pretty good on piano, if she doesn't think she's very good, her percussion must be great!' They decided to reserve judgement until they had seen the evening's performance.

In the meantime, I was taken off to see a consultant audiological physician at The London Otological Centre. Although Ann had seen the reports from my tests in Aberdeen, she felt that it would be wise to obtain a second opinion; Dr Fisch had been highly recommended by one of her contacts in the National Deaf Children's Society. The first tests were very simple; Dr Fisch asked me to move paper cups in response to the sounds of a drum which he tapped behind my back. Not a cup stirred from its place. At this point, Ann and Sandra became very depressed and when I had gone out of the room to have further electronic tests, they talked to the doctor about how I would survive in the cutthroat world of professional musicians. They were desperate to know how best to encourage me. Dr Fisch was pleasant but discouraging. I could continue some involvement with music as a hobby, but really I would be best advised to choose a rather different career. Why not become an accountant?

This was reported to me when I returned from my tests and I felt the familiar surge of indignation and sheer bloody-mindedness. An accountant! Who did they think I was! I simply replied, 'I shall just have to try harder to convince you.' The Albert Hall performance lay ahead and I would jolly well show them what was what. Fuelled by this and despite my hurt feelings, I was the least gloomy member of the rather despondent and apologetic crew which drove off to drop me at the tube station. By coincidence, Ann and Ezra had been invited to a box at the Prom, so I knew I would see them later that evening; Sandra had to go back to Aberdeen. As I stepped out on to the pavement, I remembered I had something to give Ann – a small brown envelope containing a donation I wanted to make to the Fund. She promptly burst into tears.

The performance *did* go well. By that time I was playing the main parts in the percussion group and I had a particularly good xylophone solo, which I really revelled in. I felt my usual buzz from the audience and just played away, my sticks whirling and my whole body intent on giving everything in me. For once I barely noticed the applause, my one wish was to find the Rachlins and ask them what they thought. They were sitting just in front of the stage where we were playing, but at quite a high level, and I went running round and round the back of the hall looking for their box. Finally I found it and burst in through the door, and they were both standing there looking absolutely amazed, saying, 'We were wrong, we were wrong; you've got it all and we'll do everything we can to help you.' Later Ann told me that as soon as I lifted my sticks to play, she got goose pimples up and down her arms because I looked so right; she felt at once that I had the stage presence that marks the great performer. My playing convinced them that I had a future in the music world.

Unknown to me, Sandra Buchan had been told to

phone my parents to explain the reservations that Dr Fisch and the Rachlins had about me, and Ann was now desperate to contact Sandra to cancel the bad news before she spoke to my parents. This proved slightly complicated because Sandra was on the train on the long trek north, but they did eventually get through. As always Mum and Dad were delighted, but Mum's attitude was just to take things quietly, not to get too excited, and wait and see what happened. This calm and levelheaded approach has often been useful to me, encouraging my natural instinct to work quietly and steadfastly through, rather than rushing about in a pother. Dad, of course, was secretly bursting with pride and joy.

The next step as far as the Rachlins were concerned was how best to help me, and they decided that they couldn't make any plans until they had asked the opinion of leading percussionists on my performance. Ann decided to talk to the principal percussionist of the Scottish National Orchestra, Pamela Dow, and their timpanist, Martin Gibson. But the obvious person for the Rachlins to consult was James Blades, and four months later we had our second historic meeting.

12

Never take no for an answer

After all the excitement in London, Christmas and New Year lacked their usual sparkle, although a brief concert tour in Scotland with the National Youth Orchestra of Scotland early in January helped to keep up my spirits. Of course, the local newspapers thoroughly enjoyed the opportunity to warm their readers' hearts with the story of the plucky deaf girl. Both before and after the visit to the Rachlins, we were invaded by reporters, and the local press included such emotive headlines as: 'Deaf girl tunes in to the sound of music', 'Talent triumphs over deafness', 'Persistence pays off' and 'Deaf girl on road to a musical career', most of them accompanied by a photograph of me beaming at the piano, with an admiring Hamish Park looking on! Despite my later reservations about 'sob-story' journalism, we found it tremendous fun, and I shall always be grateful for the interest and good wishes that the articles generated. All the staff at Ellon were naturally delighted with my success, and anxious for me to take advantage of the opportunities that now seemed to be opening up to me.

The Rachlins had promised to let me know as soon as they had arranged the 'audition' with James Blades, but in the meantime I pressed ahead with applications to study percussion at both the Royal Academy of Music and the Royal College of Music in London. My parents were a little troubled by this. 'Why don't you go to Glasgow?' said Mum. 'Then you'll be able to come home for the weekends.' I was still only 16 and they were naturally rather concerned at how on earth I was going to cope with the people and traffic and general busyness of London after my quiet life on the farm. But London it had to be as far as I was concerned.

I didn't mention my deafness to the Royal College, but the Royal Academy application form asked questions about my health and I was forced to confess to being deaf. The result was a rather worrying letter: 'You mention that you had or have suffered from deafness; would you please be more specific about this and tell us whether it affects your music in any way.' I did my best to reply. Unknown to me, my application sparked off quite a row at the Academy. My deafness was considered to be so serious a disadvantage that there was a strong feeling that I shouldn't even be considered as a student. Some of the staff felt that it would be irresponsible to encourage me as I had no hope of making a career for myself as a professional musician. Fortunately for me, the tutor who had first received my papers, Professor David Robinson, felt very strongly that my form gave such unmistakable evidence of musical ability that the Academy should at least invite me for an audition and find out what sort of person I was. After some nail-biting delay, I was offered an audition on 29 March, with the Royal College audition a month later.

In the meantime, I received a copy of Dr Fisch's report. I noted in my diary that I found it somewhat incomprehensible! But there was no mistaking the general implications: I was suffering from a severe loss of hearing and only my own willpower and determination enabled me to function as well as I did both in everyday conversation and as a musician. Interesting as I have always found the many tests that have been carried out on my hearing, I have never paid much attention to the subsequent reports or their recommendations. Let other people worry about it if they wanted to; my own mind was quite made up. Music was what I wanted and was my second language; as long as I could express myself musically, nothing else mattered.

At last I heard from the Rachlins. The visit to James Blades had been arranged for 21 March and I was to go down with my mother to London the previous day to stay overnight with the Rachlins. Sped on my way by the *Press and Journal*, 'Drum-roll dream trip for Evelyn', I eventually arrived at James' house just outside London at 10 am one Sunday morning. We were warmly welcomed by Joan Blades, who before her marriage had made a successful musical career as an oboist under her maiden name of Joan Goossens. Ezra and I were ushered into James' studio, a garage in the garden absolutely jampacked with percussion instruments of every variety, a magic sweetshop full of tempting goodies. In fact, I'm surprised I managed to play anything at all as my eyes kept drifting to the bells and drums, the sticks and cymbals and chimes of all shapes and sizes cramming the shelves and hanging from the ceiling.

James quickly got down to business. He cunningly began with rather simple tasks: 'Just try this. Now what about that piece? Can you sight-read? Good. Well, just play it straight through for me.' As the time went on, he gave me more and more difficult tests, trying to catch me out, but I just sailed through, even when he asked me to tune the timpani to a C. Ezra nearly leapt out of his chair at that. His mouth opened to say, 'But she's deaf!', but James motioned him to be quiet, and of course I could do it. My perfect pitch didn't let me down. Finally we played a duet on two xylophones – but back to back to see how well I could keep the beat when I couldn't see what James was playing. It all went smoothly. My years of teaching myself to read music at first sight, and all those hours of patiently counting my way through the bars at orchestra practice had paid off. Afterwards the three of us just floated out of the garage feeling completely exhilarated, and James confirmed that I must aim to obtain a place at one of the London colleges. He had been Professor of Timpani and Percussion at the Royal Academy and was now a visiting consultant, so slightly favoured that college, but felt that either of the two that I had applied for would offer a similar course and look after me well. All that remained was for me to succeed in my auditions.

I didn't see James again for some months, but he wrote after my visit to encourage me to ask Ron Forbes for more percussion pieces to practise. James' broad approach to developing the percussion repertoire and experimenting with a wide range of pieces was later to be very important to me. With his encouragement I was able to discover pieces that I just hadn't known existed. This kind of exploration and experimentation is vital to my work as a soloist.

I returned to London a week later for the Royal Academy audition. I was met by Robert Duncan, a family friend from Methlick who had studied at the Royal College, along with his twin sister Isabel, the percussionist who had first inspired my interest when she played at a local talent show all those years previously. Robert and his wife put me up for the night, and I felt rested and alert when I presented myself at the Academy the next morning. It is a stately building on the Marylebone Road, with a number of small rooms on each floor on long corridors which lead off the impressive main staircase, and busts of famous musicians on the landings. I began by having to do a written paper along with the other candidates, which was the one part of the screening procedure that I was concerned about. The paper covered both the theory and history of music and to my relief it wasn't too bad.

The practical audition wasn't until five o'clock in the afternoon, but in the meantime I managed to jam the lock of my briefcase. It had a combination lock and try as I might I couldn't get the lid to spring open. This was somewhat disastrous as the case contained the sticks and music that I wanted to use in the practical.

Eventually the porter managed to force the case open, and I went down in good time into the rabbit warren of tiny rooms in the basement to the percussion practice room where the interviewing panel was held. Nicholas Cole, the percussion teacher at the Academy, welcomed me in the corridor, which immediately made me feel relaxed. There were two other people, neither very formidable, and we had a pleasant twenty minutes or so going through my pieces. One thing that slightly threw me was that I was used to hand-tuned timpani and this was pedal-tuned, but I coped fine with that, and played the *William Tell* Overture, which has a nice busy timpani part, and then a piece on the snare drum, and the wonderful zylophone solo from Ron Forbes' Autun Carillon, which although notated sounds improvised. I knew that no one else would play this piece and the panel obviously enjoyed it. Then I played a Mozart sonata on the piano and attempted some keyboard skills and sight-reading, and ended up feeling very pleased with myself. I knew I had played my best.

The system was that if the panel were interested they would call me back for a second interview that same day, so before I left I asked, 'Is that it? Have you finished? I've a train to catch in half an hour.' The answer seemed to be 'That's it', and I thought with a little surprise, 'Oh well, I haven't managed to get in.' With true Glennie grit, however, I didn't feel disappointed. I was feeling so good about playing so well that I went happily off to King's Cross to catch my train, and had a cheerful though not particularly comfortable journey home on the night train.

When I reached Aberdeen the next morning, my mother met me and said that the Academy had rung her the previous evening to ask where I was. She had told them that I was probably on my way home, which caused great surprise. Apparently they had intended me to stay, so Mum agreed that I would see them the following month when I returned for the Royal College of Music interview. This misunderstanding caused even more problems at the Academy. The people who had been against auditioning me in the first place seized upon it as an example of the terrible problems that would ensue if they took on a deaf student, but in the end everyone realized that there had been a genuine mistake for which I wasn't to blame. Another hurdle had been crossed.

My Highers were approaching with alarming rapidity and I spent all my time over the next few weeks revising, and practising my music. The Rachlins, by now determined to help me in any way they could, had in the meantime been recruiting funds to buy me a marimba and xylophone of my own. The Beethoven Fund couldn't do this as its policy was to supply instruments that many students could use, not individuals. This didn't daunt Ann, who immediately wrote a special letter to some of the many people who had supported the Fund, drawing their attention to my need to have my own instruments. The response was impressive and within a few weeks, the Rachlins were able to enlist James Blades' help to buy the instruments. He discovered both a marimba and a xylophone that were being sold secondhand by the BBC; they were in excellent condition, so I was able to have the two for the price of one new xylophone. The two huge parcels arrived in the middle of April and I rushed to unpack and set up the instruments in my room. They took up so much space that in the end I had to move downstairs to Mum and Dad's bedroom, otherwise I might never have managed to squeeze round them into bed! These instruments are very precious to me and I still have them at home, the letters BBC still irremovably etched on the side of each.

A few days later, it was back to London for the Royal College audition and the return visit to the Academy. I went to the Academy first for a completely unprepared audition. They gave me a number of pieces on the piano that I had to play straight through by sight-reading. This time David Robinson was on the panel and he told me later that they were amazed that I could play and sight-read as sensitively as I did. There and then I had their answer: 'Why don't you start in September?' I told them that I still had to see the Royal College, but in my mind I had already decided that I would accept the Academy.

This was where fate took a hand – or maybe I should say a knee (!) – in events. It was an extremely hot day and I wandered around London feeling very relaxed and content until it was time to go to the College. I arrived a little early, but was asked to go straight in as the previous candidate had not turned up. Once again I faced a panel of three examiners, and everything went well until we came to the aural. I hadn't told them that I was deaf, so they expected me to be able to manage the usual aural tests. Of course, it was quite impossible and I finally had to confess that I couldn't hear. They were absolutely nonplussed. The last thing they had expected was a *deaf* candidate, and moreover one who could play as naturally and well as any fully hearing student. After a hurried consultation, they decided to forget the aural and told me to play my piano piece. I was unperturbed as I thought the rest of the audition had gone fine and I played as well as I could, but when I had finished and was turning to get up from the piano stool a sudden shock of pain went right through my body. I had no idea where it was coming from, but it was so excruciating that I just sat down again. I could barely speak and just kept groaning, 'Oh God', while they fluttered around me asking if I was all right.

After a moment or two I began to locate the source of the pain and groped my hand down to the hem of my skirt. My knee was jutting out at an extraordinary angle; I had managed to dislocate it as I got up from the piano stool. The next few minutes were chaotic, with me glued to the piano stool and the panel running around, ringing for an ambulance and trying to make me comfortable. The three examiners were absolutely dumbfounded. First I turn out to be deaf, then I manage to dislocate my knee. They certainly wouldn't forget me in a hurry. Apart from the pain, all I could think of was the fact that I still had to do the written paper later that afternoon. But 'You're certainly not doing that today!' and I was rushed off to the ambulance on a stretcher chair, still screaming with pain and clutching my leg, to the horror and consternation of the next candidates who were sitting outside as I was wheeled past.

Once in hospital my knee was manipulated back into place and bandaged, and I was taught how to use the crutches I would temporarily need. I was put on the next train home, with no chance to go back and tackle the written paper, and that was what finally decided me to accept the Academy. I just couldn't face the thought of any more journeys to London.

When I got home, my parents were waiting for me at Aberdeen railway station, laughing hysterically at the sight of me wobbling about on my crutches. Far from being upset, they found the story of my embarrassment hilarious, but they were delighted that I had been accepted by the Academy. Soon afterwards I had written confirmation that I could begin my studies in the autumn. Even if I didn't do well in my Highers, I could still join the Performers' course, but I was determined to get good enough grades to join the degree course and I did indeed succeed in this ambition.

The exams began only six days later, and once they were out of the way I settled down to enjoy my final weeks at home, the last time I would experience the familiar summer activities of my teenage years. Although I would not be 17 until late July, I felt that I was soon to join the world of grown-up ambitions and responsibilities, and I was putting away childish things for ever.

This did not, however, make me melancholy. There was no time for that in any case; these final months were a whirl of busy activity, beginning with a trip to Orkney with the Grampian Schools Percussion Ensemble. I had not been back to Orkney since the trip with my mother and was delighted to have the chance to enjoy its pleasant hills and beautiful coastal scenery once more. We played at St Magnus Cathedral in Kirkwall, which was where I met Sir Peter Maxwell Davies for the first time. He happened to be at the cathedral when we were rehearsing and Ron Forbes introduced us. We had a little chat and amazingly, when I met him again in June 1989 at the St Magnus Festival, he remembered having been introduced to me. My parents came with me on this trip and they went to listen to an organ recital of some of his music. Mum was not impressed. 'Sounds like me warming up,' was her opinion. They left at the interval.

I was back in Orkney again a few weeks later with the National Youth Orchestra of Scotland, for a series of concerts that took us on to the Faroe Islands, Norway, Sweden and Denmark. The Scottish composer John McLeod accompanied us, conducting his tone poem *The Gokstad Ship*. He has since then become a good friend and has composed a number of percussion pieces that are important items in my repertoire, including his Percussion Concerto and *The Song of Dionysius* which I played at my solo Prom debut in July 1989.

The summer was full of farewells: goodbye to Mrs Hunter who was still giving me piano lessons, goodbye to school and my friends and teachers there, and a farewell party with Ron Forbes and the percussion group, when they presented me with a beautiful gold necklace and bracelet. But I've always preferred beginnings to endings, and the big 'Hello' that summer was a solo performance in London in front of Prince and Princess Michael of Kent.

The Beethoven Fund for Deaf Children were holding

their third fundraising concert at the Royal Festival Hall in July. The American jazz singer Nancy Wilson and her trio were flying in specially from a run at the Carnegie Hall to give the concert, which was to be followed by a reception for the guests. Ann invited me to play at the reception, and I was delighted to accept. Mrs Cadger, the mother of my old friend Edna, made me a cream satin dress, and Mum and I set off yet again on the London train. I performed two lively pieces, Hubay's *Hejre Kati*, a Hungarian violin piece that Ron and I had arranged for percussion, and Monti's *Czardas* on the xylophone and marimba, accompanied by Ezra on the piano. Afterwards I was introduced to the royal couple and the other guests, who were most appreciative.

By now the national newspapers had begun to take an interest in me and Peta Levi's article 'Never take no for an answer', published in *The Guardian* on the morning of the Beethoven Fund reception, made me feel that at last I was on my way to recognition as a serious musician. But I knew too that, despite all the applause and praise, I was only at the beginning. Ahead of me lay three years of gruelling work to achieve mastery of my instruments and to prepare myself for my future as a professional. Anything might happen in that time and the outcome was still uncertain. All I knew was that I was going to work like crazy. The desire to succeed was firmly lodged in my heart, and nothing was going to stop me.

13

Beginning a new chapter

'I believe art is born, not of "I can", but of
"I must"!'

Arnold Schoenberg

In my diary for 19 September 1982 I noted, 'Got up
early and caught the 7.30 am train to London to start
my studies at the RAM. It's like beginning a new chap-
ter.' My parents came to see me off at Aberdeen railway
station, the first of their children to live what seemed
to be so far away. As I waved goodbye to their bravely
smiling faces, I knew that the one thought in their minds
was that they would not be able to speak to me again
until Christmas. We would just have to make do with
letters and phone calls via the new friends I hoped I
would make in London.

The eight-hour journey gave me a chance to sort out
the confusion of thoughts rushing through my mind
and to make some serious plans for the future. First
and foremost was the determination to make the most
of my time in 'smoke city'. I had no idea what standards
of performance and musical ability I would find among
my fellow students, but I decided it would be best to
regard them all as excellent and dedicated musicians. I
was going to have to work hard to meet these standards
and to make progress both as a musician and as a
person. I knew exactly what I intended to achieve in
my playing, and was particularly keen to develop the
possibilities of performing solo percussion. I was also

looking forward to meeting the other students at the hostel and all the important-sounding teachers whose names I had studied in the prospectus. There would be so much to learn and experience and I wasn't going to allow the three years to slip through my fingers like so much sand. As far as I was concerned, London was the place for me, but I could forget the idea of bright lights and discos. I was here to study and study hard.

With these stern but inspiring resolves fresh in my thoughts, I made my way cheerfully from King's Cross station to the Academy hostel, Ethel Kennedy Jacobs House in Camberwell, a leafy suburb in south-east London. I needed my good humour, for the journey was appalling, heaving bulky bags and suitcases on and off tubes and buses in a summer heatwave. I arrived totally exhausted. 'Ethel's' was a big old house surrounded by trees in pleasant grounds. The hostel offered rather a chilly environment, with a sparsely equipped communal living room and a shared kitchen which I quickly learnt to avoid, as it was invariably littered with bits of everyone's food and uncleared-up rubbish. I was extremely fortunate in my bedroom, a double room on the first floor, large enough to cope with my ever-increasing collection of percussion instruments and with pleasant views in winter out over the snow-laden trees. The girl who should have shared it with me never turned up, so I was able to practise (quietly) to my heart's content and to develop my own living routines. As I have always kept my Hillhead habit of getting up soon after six, this was perhaps just as well! Being alone has no horrors for me; the space to think and potter and organize my work is incredibly important, and once I had left Ethel's to share a flat in my second year, my diary again and again notes my joy when I managed to have the place to myself.

The hostel housed about fifty first-year Academy students, so we were able to help one another to adjust to our new life of looking after ourselves and learning how to make our way around London. On the day of my arrival, we all crammed into the living room for a 'getting-to-know-you' session. When it was my turn to introduce myself, everyone went 'Oh!' as they had seen the publicity about my acceptance at the Academy. With all these high-spirited boys and girls about the place, the warden had a terrible time, with constant practical jokes to make his life difficult. Sometimes he would find stacks of furniture blocking the doorway to his office, or the door handle would be covered with cooking grease, and his furniture and even the trees outside were frequently festooned with toilet paper. I kept away from these pranks and was glad to be free of the noise and disruption when I left Ethel's the following summer.

My first day at the Academy got off to a good start. I travelled in with a crowd of students from Ethel's. In fact I soon came to enjoy the hour's trip in from Denmark Hill, a chance to collect my thoughts and take note of my fellow passengers. It was my first experience of the many different races who make up London's population, and I found myself staring particularly at the unfamiliar black faces with an interest that sometimes led to a hostile response. 'Hey man, what you staring at?' I learnt to be more discreet.

The professor for percussion was Nicholas Cole, who was also the principal percussionist with the Royal Philharmonic Orchestra. My first impression of Nick was of a gentle, soft-spoken man, whom I privately described as rather cuddly. Needless to say, I kept this opinion to myself and was still addressing him formally as Mr Cole long after the other new students were calling him Nick. Like the other two (male) percussionists in my year, I had weekly private lessons with Nick. James Blades was still a visiting teacher at the Academy and gave each of us a lesson once or twice a term. But perhaps inevitably a lot of the hard grind of practising and developing percussion techniques and repertoire had to be done on my own in any practice space I could find.

My principal frustration at the Academy was the fact that I never seemed to have as much teaching or practice time as I would have liked to work at pieces, or to learn how to exploit to the full the many different percussion instruments that I was studying. One of the problems was possibly the sheer variety of instruments. I was working on the xylophone, vibraphone, marimba, snare drum, timpani, and orchestral instruments, to name but a few. Although I began to build up my own collection of sticks and beaters, and some of the smaller instruments during my first year, my xylophone and marimba weren't brought down to London until February of my third year. Before that I was dependent on the instruments and practice rooms provided by the Academy.

There were usually about eleven percussion students studying at the Academy at any one time, and we all shared the small percussion room in the basement where I had had my two auditions. This room was used for classes as well as practice and, as most of the classes were one-to-one, the time available for me to use the room was limited. When the room was free, two or three of us would be squashed in there at one time, beating away, until the inevitable knock on the door: 'Can you stop for a while? We've a concert on.' The percussion room was situated directly below the main theatre and recital room where the various orchestras rehearsed and master classes were held. It was next door to the recording studio and directly opposite the concert room which was used for lunch-time concerts, exams and competitions. Predictably, the sound-proofing in the room left a lot to be desired, so we could be heard all over the building when we were in full beat! Luckily for me, I was able to switch off from everything around me and just concentrate on what I was receiving from my own instruments, but it was frequently pandemonium.

113

Throughout my three years at the Academy, the practice situation was a nightmare. At one stage I even considered taking my drumkit and busking in the tube, just to get in some undisturbed playing. I often stayed until the college closed at 8.45 in the evening, by which time there were usually only two other students there, a keen violinist and a cellist, so we weren't competing for rooms. I liked to have a room with a mirror so I could watch how I was playing. I also went in early and sometimes managed to play before the official practice time began at 9 am. Alternatively I played in the corridor or in the extraordinarily long thin washroom in the Ladies, which provided excellent elbow room. After a few days of this, up would go the notices: 'Students are expressly forbidden to practise in the corridors. . . .' I would nip in on my 8 am forays and tear them down. All this corridor practice did mean that I got noticed. On one occasion a harmony lecturer commented on how beautiful a Bach chorale sounded adapted for the marimba. He hadn't known Bach could be played on this instrument. A visitor on a tour of the building spoke glowingly to Nick Cole of 'the outstanding brilliance of the percussionist'. This was obligingly reported to me and cheered me up for several days.

Percussion was not the whole of my studies. I attended classes in the history and theory of music with other students in my year. The staff were all aware of my deafness and, as at Ellon, did their best to speak clearly and face the class. However, my deafness was so unapparent that they quickly forgot and would rattle on at an incredible speed about all sorts of unfamiliar topics, whilst my eyes were working overtime to watch their faces and scribble notes at the same time. Even the hearing students had difficulties with some of the staff, who liked to use as many long and incomprehensible words as possible. This became particularly problematic in my third year as the time for finals approached, and I became quite exhausted with the effort to keep up with what was going on in class. This, rather than the practical aspects of music, was when my deafness really troubled me.

I continued to work at the piano, and it became almost as major an instrument as percussion. My teacher, Graeme Humphrey, rapidly became a great favourite. Not only was he young and extremely handsome, he was a born teacher and appeared to have a good understanding of his students' needs and behaviour. Piano lessons were a highlight of my week as Graeme pushed me to improve my skills. I had neither the talent nor the wish to become a first-rate pianist, but I did want to be good enough to perform the keyboard part in any percussion composition. I also wanted to be able to play the piano accompaniment to percussion solos so that I would have as full an understanding as possible of the music. In fact, in my 1989 solo Prom I did play the piano as well as percussion in John McLeod's *The Song of Dionysius*. By the end of my first year I had decided to do piano as a first study as well as percussion. Very few students did two first studies for their degree, so it was an interesting challenge, and it would also boost my overall degree result if I did well. I had by this time already made up my mind that three years at the Academy would be enough and was working to cram as much knowledge as I could into my pre-degree years.

Timothy Baxter taught me harmony and counterpoint. We would sit side by side pouring over music scores and working out how the different parts related. Since losing my hearing, I have also lost my ability to sing, although I can speak like any normally hearing person, but during my first lesson Timothy asked me to sing the opening bars of Beethoven's *Eroica* Symphony. Politely I explained that I couldn't sing, but I wrote the music down for him, to his great surprise. Even when the staff were aware that they had a deaf student in their midst, they didn't know quite how my deafness operated and what kinds of techniques I had developed to compensate, and it took a little time for them to understand that I could manage almost anything if allowed to work problems out in my own way. There was a lot of homework for the harmony lesson, so I spent many hours in the library, studying Bach scores in particular. Harmonizing Bach's chorales and understanding his technique were enormously important as he was such a master of voicings and harmony, and I would also experiment by harmonizing one of his soprano or bass parts in the style of a contemporary composer.

Because I couldn't do aural tests I studied keyboard skills instead. These included reading orchestral and vocal scores, playing them on the piano, transposing music for different instruments, sight-reading and identifying music by various composers. It was not a subject I felt very comfortable with, but my three years with DR taught me a lot. DR was none other than Professor David Robinson, who had fielded my application through all the objections placed in its path. He was also the head tutor for the degree students and taught stylistic analysis classes in my third year. We got on like a house on fire and I always looked forward to our work together. He was so patient and gentle, and always interested and full of encouragement for everything I did. I became tremendously fond of him and thought that if he had been twenty years younger – and not married to his extremely pleasant wife – he would have been the man for me! Of course I never told him this, but I hope my beams of enjoyment let him know how much I appreciated his kindness and help.

Much as I enjoyed these parts of my course, there was one aspect that I hated more and more. The Academy had a number of orchestras which included the 'training' orchestra for first-year students, the repertoire orchestra which aimed to develop knowledge of classical repertoire, and the symphony orchestra which simply aimed at excellence in its players. There was also the opera orchestra, sinfonia and other small ensembles. As there were three percussionists in my year, we each had one term playing timpani and two terms on percussion in whatever orchestra we were practising with. Attendance at rehearsals for the various orchestras was compulsory and ate an enormous bite out of each week. What was particularly frustrating was that many of the pieces required little input from the percussion section, and week after week I would spend hours hanging around waiting until it was my turn to contribute my eight notes. This drove me absolutely crazy. What I wanted was to be making a contribution and having an audience respond to my performance. It was not enough for me to pop in with a little bit here and there; I wanted to be a star! As a result, when I did get the chance to play, I would make the most of it and was often rather guiltily aware of going 'over the top' with my flamboyant presentation.

My orchestral experience was not wasted, however. I began to understand the art of orchestral playing as opposed to just learning the pieces. I learnt how orchestral pieces were put together and how the various instrumental sections interacted. I began to realize how important it is for the orchestra to function as one instrument, and my playing became more controlled and thoughtful. This valuable experience was mainly the result of working with our principal conductor Maurice Handford, who was sadly to die of cancer after I had left the Academy. We also had guest conductors such as Antal Dorati; 'Such a tonic!' I wrote in my diary after working with him on one occasion. Simon Rattle thought I must be an aspiring conductor myself because of the flattering way in which I watched his every move. 'Oh no,' said a colleague; 'Evelyn *has* to watch your mouth. She's deaf!' He was most surprised. Another conductor is reported to have asked anxiously whether Ms Glennie was a bit slow in the head. He was apparently wondering why I had failed to respond to remarks addressed to me whilst I was crawling on the floor looking for an errant drumstick. It was suggested that he tried talking to my face not my bum.

Learning to read music quickly and efficiently was an essential part of orchestral playing as well as solo work. Before a rehearsal, I would study a score so that I knew all the parts, and could imagine how the conductor was likely to work with the music. I learnt to read vertically rather than horizontally during rehearsals, so that I could see at a glance how all the sections related. I couldn't, of course, study by listening to tapes or records of music; I must have been the only student at the Academy who didn't use the listening room. What I had to do was to teach myself to read music like a book, and the only way to do this was by constant study, usually on the bus or tube on my way into college. For solo performances, I have to know the music off by heart so that I can concentrate on the instrument not on looking at sheets of paper. It's the only way I know whether I am playing a wrong note. The advantages of my method of 'private' study is that I am not influenced by other performers' interpretations of a work. Everything I play is 'Evelyn'. I work through to my own feelings for the piece and come to know every detail both of the notation and its expression.

The frustration I felt at being such an unimportant member of the orchestral team encouraged me to revive my earlier ideas about trying to develop as a soloist. At that time in the UK, solo percussionists were almost unheard of, although there were a number in the USA, and *female* solo percussionists hardly existed. Nicholas Cole's view, quoted in an article in the magazine *Classical Music* in June 1982 just before I joined the Academy, was: 'You couldn't make your living as a solo player any more than you could on the tuba.' There was no precedent for it, partly because the repertoire of pieces for solo percussion was so small.

Looking back on it, I can understand why Nick was so cautious. Here was this young girl determined to break new ground, but the staff were quite accustomed to students entering the Academy with enormous ambitions which often didn't come off. They just had to take a cool view of it all and see how I got on, but the problems with the percussion repertoire and the sheer cost of ferrying the range of instruments around the country and abroad for solo recitals seemed serious deterrents to my crusade. It would be irresponsible to encourage me to look for a professional career outside the two outlets conventionally available: orchestral performance and teaching.

Since then I've travelled in Europe, Japan and America, experiencing the work of other solo players and developing my repertoire, and have had a number of pieces composed especially for me. Percussion itself has become better recognized, with a proper syllabus and graded examinations for children. As David Robinson recently said to me, in twenty years time I'll probably be able to look back and say, 'What a lot of wonderful music has been written.' But at the time, I sometimes felt I was fighting a lonely and rather dispiriting battle with only my sheer bolshiness to keep me going.

My dedicated and innovative approach did not endear me to my fellow percussionists, who were a relaxed bunch and happy to 'toe the party line'. They were envious of the fact that I practised so hard, and were occasionally unhelpful in orchestral rehearsals, shrugging their shoulders if I asked them to repeat a comment from the conductor that I hadn't followed. As I was also no drinker and didn't like to socialize in noisy and smoky pubs, I became increasingly isolated from my peers, and spent more and more time on my own in the library or practising wherever I could find a corner and a suitable instrument. I wasn't happy about this situation and went over and over it in my head, wondering what I had done wrong and whether

I was truly selfish and not worth knowing. In the end I came to understand that survival for some people means huddling in groups and finding support in following each other's behaviour. This was not my way. I wanted to be strong and independent, and not to risk jeopardizing my goals by worrying about other folks' opinions. As my determination grew, so did my confidence, and I stopped agonizing over the hostile behaviour I encountered.

It wasn't all doom and gloom, however. The rest of my musical development was rushing forward, and with the help of James Blades I at last began to see how I could make some progress towards my dream of making a name for myself as a solo player. When he visited the Academy, he would put us through a gruelling programme of sight-reading and playing techniques on a variety of instruments. He would spice our meetings with stories of his work with Chaplin and Benjamin Britten, making me roar with laughter at his ingenious experiments to try to produce exactly the right sound effect.

'Britten said to me, "I want a *wham*, Jim; I don't want a bell and I don't want a gong. You know what I want." When a man like Britten says "You know what I want", what do you do? You go and get it, so I had it specially made at a foundry. "Marvellous, Jim – order me a spare." '

Despite his 80 years, James was totally up-to-date with techniques and repertoire, and urged me to delve into both these areas as deeply as possible. Like all my teachers he was curious about exactly how I could manage to play and hear music, and he was keen to push me on as far as I could go. We would sight-read duets together on the snare drum and out would come his elbow to nudge me if I made any mistakes. As I came to know him better, I would give my own fair share of nudges if I felt him 'slipping it off'. We became extremely fond of one another, and I was inspired both his musicianship and infectious enthusiasm, and by his sheer love of people, whatever their age, sex, colour or background, qualities that I particularly enjoyed when we travelled to America together three years later. The idea was James' of course, and he first began to suggest it to me some time in my second year. In the meantime, he offered help of a characteristically practical nature.

I had quickly discovered the percussion section in the library, and was determined to sort out my percussion techniques, using music that I photocopied from the books and scores that I could find there. However, the library could only provide a limited range of often dusty works for me to study, and I became increasingly greedy to learn more about what was available for percussion. Here James provided invaluable help. He introduced me to magazines and journals, many from the USA, which dealt with percussion, and encouraged me to write away for music catalogues and information about sticks and instruments. Often when I ordered music, the pieces that arrived were not entirely suitable for what I was looking for, but at least I was discovering that there was a considerably larger body of material available than I had at first thought, and I was beginning to see how broad a musical range the percussion family offered: contemporary, jazz, Latin, classical, rags and blues, folk, and so on. I felt eager to try them all, and began to develop my own repertoire of 'popular' numbers, as well as the solos I adapted from music by Bach, Mozart, Vivaldi and the other great masters. I established my own little corner in the library where I could study and dream to my heart's content, feeling increasingly confident that I would attain my passionate desire: Evelyn Glennie, professional *solo* percussionist.

14

My horizons expand

'As far as the execution is concerned . . . one might say that the most frequent and most serious mistake is to follow the music instead of preceding it.'

Nadia Boulanger

By the end of my first term at the Academy, I was dying to be home. Mum always wrote two or three times a week and sent me the little treats that I missed so much, homemade marmalade and fresh sweet carrots from our garden, but I was longing to see them all for a good relaxed 'news' in our familiar tongue, and to breathe some clean fresh air. My time in London had been entirely preoccupied with practicalities, getting from A to B on time, and I had barely noticed a bird or tree for months. Back at the farm I could stop being responsible grown-up Evelyn, and recapture the freedom and openness of a child. The house was warm with a glorious glowing fire, and the countryside gleamed with snow and the scattered dots of light from neighbouring farms. I revelled in the wide open spaces around me – I was home.

I was not allowed to rusticate for long. On 22 December I heard that I had been voted Scot of the Year for 1982. The award was organized by BBC Radio Scotland's *Good Morning Scotland* programme, and once a year listeners were invited to nominate the Scot whom they felt deserved the title for outstanding achievement. I was astonished that so many people who were strangers to me had shown such an interest in my life, and was tremendously honoured and encouraged that my fellow Scots had taken my to their hearts.

I had an exciting trip by train to Edinburgh a few days later to receive an engraved crystal glass and be interviewed by Neville Garden, a well-known voice on BBC Radio Scotland and one that my family had been listening to every morning for years. The newspapers sent reporters and cameras, and I had a wonderful time dealing with all their questions and posing at a piano with the trophy in my hand. Later that day I walked up our bumpy farm road with the precious crystal in a box under my arm, just as if it were a new pair of shoes!

Soon after this I was invited to appear on a live chat show on Scottish television, *Friday Night with Dougie Donnelly*. 'Not bad for a beginner', I wrote in my diary. Although I had hoped to play percussion, they were very keen for me to perform one of my own compositions on the piano, Wishing, which I had written at Ellon. As this was my first television performance, I wasn't going to argue; Wishing is a light, nostalgic, rather romantic piece, which audiences always seem to love. I took tremendous care with my personal presentation, scouring the London shops for weeks beforehand for a suitable outfit, for which I paid the vast sum of £37.90! I bought a pretty, light mauve dress, and felt confident that the colour and image would come across well on the screen.

I flew to Glasgow for the show on 17 March. It was a big adventure for me as I had never flown alone before, and had no experience of how to get to Heathrow airport. As for what would happen at the other end, well, I would just have to deal with it when I got there. I arrived safely at Heathrow on the tube, but was overwhelmed by the sheer size of the place and the volume of people standing in queues, browsing in the shops, or just milling around in an apparently aimless fashion. I was determined to handle the trip without asking other people for help, so was relieved to see that there was a screen to give information about departures. I had been dreading broadcast announcements. Once in Glasgow, it was all smooth sailing. I was met at the airport and taken to the studio to meet Dougie and the crew. The other two guests were Herbie Flowers from the group Sky, and the rock singer Maggie Bell. I had already met Tristan Fry, the percussionist from Sky, so felt at home with Herbie, and Dougie was a charming character, who treated me with great kindness and respect.

We rehearsed all afternoon for the final recording, which was made one hour before transmission, so there was no room for any mistakes. I was interested in the technical details – the lights, cameras, sound, positioning and so on, and barely noticed the heat and hard work. The show went very well, with a relaxed and pleasant interview with Dougie after I had played. Afterwards we all sat and watched it together before I was checked into the poshest hotel I had ever experienced, the Grosvenor in Glasgow. It was plush and cosy and I adored every minute of the experience. But despite my comfy bed, I could hardly sleep for excitement. The show had gone as well as it possibly could, and I had managed every step of the journey and my television appearance as if I had perfect hearing. This was an enormous relief and gave my confidence a terrific boost. The next day I wandered around Glasgow airport completely unfussed about the journey home, and enjoying the novelty of being recognized by people who had watched the show. My first experience of stardom!

To my great delight, over the next few weeks letters from 'fans' crammed my pigeonholes at the hostel and Academy, and I was kept busy writing brief thank-yous to everyone to express my appreciation. I also received other invitations from BBC radio and magazines such as *Women's Realm* keen to do features on me. I decided that I would accept these invitations so long as they didn't interfere with the time I needed for study, and provided that I could ensure that the interviews stressed my musicianship and not my deafness. With these provisos, I plunged happily into the new opportunities for publicity and thoroughly enjoyed gaining experience of handling the media.

This was not my first visit to Glasgow and I was to make several visits to the city during my student years. The Scottish National Orchestra were based there and I made a number of appearances with them, staying with the percussionist Pamela Dow, who became a great friend. I also visited two scientists, Dr Lionel Naftalin and Dr Laszlo Juhasz, who had research experience in hearing problems. Dr Naftalin had read about me in the newspaper accounts of my contact with the Beethoven Fund and wrote to Ann Rachlin to express his interest, sending her examples of his research papers. Ann suggested that he should see me in person, and he and Dr Juhasz carried out a variety of tests at Strathclyde University in Glasgow. While it was difficult to be absolutely certain, they concluded that the problem lay in the inner ear, probably with the sensory cells. Although tests on my brain activity indicated no response to speech, they did show a reaction to musical sound. The two scientists believe that this is because the energy transmitted by a musical signal is many times greater than that of speech and is therefore easier for the hearing mechanism and nervous system to pick up. Because these are the only sounds that my brain can identify, I have become increasingly sensitive to musical signals over the years; my 'musicality', the fact that I am naturally receptive to music, has also helped.

Interesting as I found my sessions with the two scientists and fond as I became of both of them, I never hoped that they would discover some miraculous cure for my hearing. I was happy to cooperate with their experiments and glad if what they discovered might be useful for other deaf people, but it didn't disappoint me to learn that no surgery or hearing aid currently available was going to restore me to good hearing. I had learnt to cope with my silent world, and felt that my own ways of listening to music gave me a sensitivity that I far preferred to the 'normal' way of hearing that I had experienced as a tiny child. Because I had to concentrate with every fibre of my body and brain, I experienced music with a profundity that I felt was God-given and precious. I didn't want to lose that special gift.

As I gained confidence in handling my musical studies, I began to look around me in London and to enjoy what the city had to offer. I had never before paid to attend a concert given by other people, and soon made my way to the Queen Elizabeth Hall to see the Fires of London performing works composed and conducted by Sir Peter Maxwell Davies. My attention was riveted by their percussionist, Gregory Knowles, who was using techniques that I had never seen before. I went to see the ensemble many times after that and continued to appreciate Gregory's great style, and active and involved performance.

I also began to attend rehearsals by leading orchestras such as the London Symphony, the London Philharmonic and the Royal Philharmonic. I would take along the score and use the opportunity to familiarize myself with the music. By the time of the actual performance, I knew it off by heart and could concentrate on the orchestra's performance and presentation. I was keen to observe how the different sections communicated with the conductor and in particular how soloists interacted with the orchestra and conductor, and to take note of basic rehearsal techniques. The rehearsals took place in some of London's most prestigious concert halls, such as the Royal Festival Hall and the Barbican, and time after time I would whisper to myself, 'One day, I will play here.' I wasn't alarmed by these venues; the vast spaces would give me a burning, excited feeling, and I would often stay alone in the hall after everyone had gone to enjoy the silence and then the magical image of myself performing. These experiences were a tremendous medicine for how I thought about myself and for my growth as a musician.

Despite my problems with my fellow percussionists at the Academy, my social life was also expanding. I have always enjoyed one-to-one relationships as I so much enjoy the opportunity to communicate deeply with people and find out how they 'tick'. I also have no reservations about who I talk to, and am happy to 'news' with anyone if I feel that we get on. Very early in my time at the Academy I made friends with the roadsweeper who was usually cleaning up the street outside the entrance as I arrived to get in some early practice. Ben was a friendly and intelligent man, who enjoyed chatting to the passers-by. We would some-times go for coffee at Baker Street tube station, and chatter about our life and plans. He even bought me a box of chocolates for Christmas, which I told him off about: 'Keep your pennies for yourself!'

Another friend was a young policeman whom I met on the train down from Scotland, and I became attached to a fellow musician in my first year at the Academy. Unfortunately, my romantic relationships with men were never very satisfactory at this time. I just didn't feel that I had time to meet every day for meals or visits to the pub and cinema, and when I made this clear to boyfriends it always seemed to cause bad feeling. As I looked around me I saw many couples at the college whose time for study and practice was controlled by when they would next meet. I never felt that there were enough hours in the day to do all I wanted, and wasn't prepared to have my time any further scheduled than it already was. I felt sad that this decision usually seemed to mean that I had to say goodbye to a friendship, and worried that I was being selfish, but I felt that the time for a steady relationship would be when I was nearer to achieving my goals. In the meantime, I wanted to be free to enjoy all the new people and opportunities that came my way, and every day seemed to open up new possibilities.

Whenever I could, I played with ensembles and orchestras outside the Academy at concerts in and around London, and performed at 'gigs' with other musicians from the Academy. These concerts were sometimes inconvenient. I had to leave a week early during the Easter holiday in my first year to rehearse with The Music Ensemble for several concerts in and around London. Of course I could have turned down the offer, but my thinking was, 'This may well be what it's like when you're a professional musician. You'd just better get used to it!' Mum was terribly disappointed, and I felt sad to leave my family after such a short time with them, but the concerts were worthwhile, and the week alone at the hostel was blissful. For once I could practise as much as I wanted – and on the best piano, too! – and, miraculously, none of my food went missing.

I was usually paid at least expenses and sometimes a fee for my performances, and enjoyed the opportunity to develop my skills in front of an audience, even if I only had a few bars to play. I was saving hard to buy music and instruments so every penny helped, and I also took the opportunity to inform the organizers and conductors that I was mainly interested in solo work. If they ever considered programming a percussion concerto, they should bear me in mind. The reactions were predictable but discouraging: '*Are* there any concertos for percussion?' I had an uphill task ahead of me to change this kind of negativism.

One of these conversations coincided with a particularly boring patch in the Academy orchestra. One day I wrote furiously in my diary: 'Had the most aggravat-

Above: My parents, Isobel and Arthur Glennie, on their wedding day, 1959.

Left: Important guests at the wedding, Grandma and Granpa Howie.

Below: In my huge pram on the farm, aged one.

With my brothers, Roger and Colin, 1968.

On to bigger and better stages: the Cults Percussion Ensemble (I am on the far right) at the Fairfield Halls, Croydon, 1978.

Right: June 1982: with Ann Rachlin at a reception at which I played following a concert in aid of the Beethoven Fund for Deaf Children at the Royal Festival Hall.

Below: At the Royal Academy of music, 1984, at the age of eighteen. Being taken through my strokes by John Chimes.

Above: July 1984: during the Shell/LSO Scholarship Week, at Masterclass with John Chimes, timpanist with the BBC Symphony Orchestra, Michael Frye, at that time principal percussionist with the London Symphony Orchestra, and Kurt-Hans Goedicke, principal timpanist with the London Sympany Orchestra.

Left: February 1984: working on a 'Highway' programme at Crathie church, Deeside.

Above: Sunday 8 July 1984: celebrating with Andrzej Panufnik after winning the Schell/LSO Percussion Scholarship.

Left: Sharing a joke with James Blades in Disneyland, Los Angeles, November 1985.

Above: July 1986: at the House of Commons with Edward Heath, receiving the travel scholarship from 'Opportunities for the Disabled'.

Right: Using Ernie Wise's head as a drum at the Mayfair Hotel, 1987.

Above: With composer John McLeod at the Eden Court Theatre in Inverness, 1987.

Left: With Sian Edwards in Newcastle, 1989.

Above: In Rio de Janeiro for *Carnaval*, February 1989: members of the *Samba* school in our blue, silver and white costumes, preparing for the one-hour non-stop parade.

Right: Drumming out the beat on my snare drum.

ing day you could ever wish to have. I spent three hours in orchestras doing absolutely nothing. I was so furious. Everyone's just forcing me to play in an orchestra and they all think that playing in one is the most important thing a musician can do. I'm going to show them all that I can be and *am* a soloist.' Quite a fiery entry, but there were days when I would just sit there and never lift a single stick.

To prepare myself for the hoped-for breakthrough, I was quietly working on the percussion repertoire, keeping myself going with visions of one day playing a substantial piece with one of the Academy orchestras. This never happened because the conductors weren't aware of what was available and thought that hiring parts from the States would be expensive; they were also reluctant to spend time rehearsing a range of instruments that they considered unsuitable for solo prominence. In the meantime I plugged away, studying the Concertino for Marimba written by the American composer Paul Creston in 1940, which I had dug up in the library. This was the first marimba concerto that I had so far attempted and I spent a considerable part of my practice time on it during my second term.

Soon after I found a second marimba concerto by another American composer, Robert Kurka, who died of leukaemia when he was only 35; 'quite nice, very jazzy . . . yeah!' was how I described it. This piece was technically more stretching than any I had previously encountered as it required virtuoso four-mallet playing. I had barely played before with four mallets, a technique where you hold two mallets in each hand, positioned between the fingers so that each mallet strikes a different note. I decided that the only way to master the piece was to learn the notes off by heart so that I could concentrate all my efforts on watching the movement of the mallets to see whether I was hitting the right notes. I have been working on this piece at odd moments ever since, but only finally felt I had brought it to performance standard in 1989. It is an easy piece to play badly with lots of inaccurate notes, but extraordinarily difficult to produce exactly the sounds the composer intended. My work on it has certainly done wonders for my four-mallet technique.

My attempts to gain a voice as a percussionist might be lonely and somewhat unrewarding at this time, but my piano playing offered the warm and supportive environment I craved. Graeme would hold lessons in the early evening where a group of students could play scales and full-length pieces to one another, and I loved having the opportunity both to perform and to listen to others, and comment on and analyze our work together. This informal meeting of committed students gave me insight into something that was very precious to me; not only could I appreciate the technical abilities of my fellow pianists, but I could also discover their true musicianship, that extra quality that came from deep inside the heart.

The Rachlins continued to be good friends, encouraging my music and introducing me to other young people who had also had to overcome hearing problems. One of these was Jessica Rees. A charming and brilliant girl, Jessica had been totally deaf since early childhood, but had still managed to obtain a place as an undergraduate at Oxford. Another was Paul Whittaker, an organist who had been partially deaf from birth. Paul was elected to associate membership of the Royal College of Organists, after a campaign to persuade the College to substitute their standard aural examination with a test appropriate for a deaf student. Paul and I played together on a number of occasions, including Wadham College in Oxford where he was studying and in Huddersfield at concerts in aid of the Beethoven Fund, and we've become good friends.

I particularly remember the Huddersfield event. I was giving my usual electrifying performance of *Hejre Kati* when the head of one of my xylophone sticks went flying off into the audience! I decided to make a comedy out of it and stayed calm. Tristan Fry of Sky was also on the bill and it was great to chat to him again. We became good friends and used to meet up whenever he was appearing in London, and he was super about lending me instruments for concerts. So often I would turn up and find that the hire company had provided a real dud. Their attitude seemed to be, 'She's deaf; she won't hear it's a bad instrument,' and along would come some dreadful old marimba, out of tune or with no resonance. All I could do in that situation was to adapt my marimba parts to the lower end of the xylophone and refuse to pay the hire bill, but it was tremendously annoying and meant I just couldn't sound my best. On one occasion two out of the four instruments I had hired were unusable, which meant replanning my entire repertoire. For a solo recital due to start in three hours, this was pretty hair-raising!

When I look back over my musical career, I sometimes find myself musing over the inevitable question, 'What if?' What if I hadn't played the piano at Aberdeen's Cowdray Hall all those years ago, what if my parents had insisted on sending me to the deaf school, what if Ron Forbes had not detected my percussion potential, what if Sandra Buchan hadn't written to the Rachlins, or the Academy had turned me down? The list is endless and I try not to dwell too much on the implications. Somehow or other God just seems to have been on my side at these crucial moments. Towards the end of my first year I experienced another example of these seemingly chance happenings that was to have a profound effect on my musical career.

The Japanese performer Keiko Abe is one of the world's foremost marimbists. By a stroke of good fortune she gave a master class that June at the Royal College of Music. Although I had never heard of her and knew nothing of the concert, I was taken along by a friend and was immediately overwhelmed by her performance and technique. Not only did she introduce me to new repertoire, she was also an exceptional communicator, and opened my eyes to the possibilities of the marimba. She saw it as an instrument in its own right, and from then on I knew I could do something special, not just with the marimba, but with percussion as a whole.

Afterwards one of the percussionists who had attended the class commented, 'There's no hope of us ever achieving that standard – it's just out of our reach.' Those words are still engraved on my mind. 'What an attitude,' I said to myself; I was determined to prove him wrong. Hungry for knowledge, restless to travel and exchange ideas with players who shared my enthusiasm for the boundless possibilities of percussion, I resolved there and then that I would seek her out. One day I was going to be taught by Keiko Abe. The £5 entrance fee seemed exceptionally well spent.

My pleasure at Keiko's master class was a fitting end for my first year at the Academy. I returned home to another kind of happiness. Romeo, a young Philippine singer whom I had met at the Aberdeen International Festival of Music and the Performing Arts in July 1981, returned to perform again that summer with his choir. I was overjoyed to see him and felt that despite our time apart we were as close as ever. We had written to each other over the two years, but there was still a lot of news to exchange.

Seeing Romeo made me realize how important it is for me to feel the genuine, loving, caring side of people. It felt very peaceful to have someone who meant so much to me all to myself, and I could try to express my loving feelings towards him in my words and actions. My parents were very taken with him and he spent two happy evenings with us on the farm. I took a photo of the three of them sitting on the settee together, Romeo so handsome and exotic in contrast to my rather sober-looking mum and dad. Romeo even talked about marrying after our studies were finished and, although it seemed to me an incredible idea – I still thought of the world as a huge area where people were very different from one another – I was heartbroken when we had to part. We made many promises about writing and about how we would work hard over the years of separation until we could be together for good. We knew, too, that we were both at an age where we were always meeting new people and where curiosity was strong; we had still to mature and so much could happen. In fact, we did continue to write for several years, but eventually our contact dwindled and I haven't heard from him for some time now. Fortunately, on that sunny August day, we didn't guess that we wouldn't meet again – and I still expect Romeo's smiling face to pop up at some recital or other.

My consolation for this separation was the prospect of performing at another Beethoven Fund reception in November. This time the Duchess of Gloucester would be present, and Ezra was to accompany me once more. Mum and I sped around, buying purple satin which Edna's mother, Mrs Cadger, made into a long dress for me. The fittings were something of a trial, as I was forced to stand like a dummy with the inevitable pins scratching me at every false move. Worse than an orchestra rehearsal!

Going back to London in the train, I made my by now customary review of progress and settled my resolutions for year two at the Academy. Work, work, work was of course on the agenda. Having seen what Keiko Abe was capable of, I knew that I too could become a percussion soloist but it would mean total dedication. Unlike Keiko, I didn't want to specialize in one instrument, but to be a 'world' percussionist. I needed to expand my repertoire and to develop my ability to handle four-mallet techniques so that I could attempt more ambitious and substantial pieces. I also wanted to continue my piano playing, and to progress with the theoretical studies. My busy thoughts made the journey whizz past. I had a will to win; what I wanted now were results.

15

A will to win

'I pay no attention whatever to anybody's praise or blame ... I simply follow my own feelings.'

Wolfgang Amadeus Mozart

A major preoccupation at the beginning of my second year was to find somewhere suitable to live. In September I moved into a flat in Archway in North London with two cellists from the Academy. The flat was tiny, cold and uninspiring, but at least I had a room to myself. Unfortunately the cellists did not see eye to eye, and I seemed to be the shoulder that they both cried on, no matter how much I tried to keep out of things. Finally one of the girls couldn't stand it any longer and left; we replaced her with a non-musician. Liz worked in a bookshop, which meant that Jo and I had the flat to ourselves most of the day.

An elderly couple lived on the ground floor beneath us, so I wasn't able to practise as freely as I wished, but I did have a small rubber practice pad which I used to improve my drumwork. I was happily beating away on this one evening, when I felt a terrible banging on the door. Mrs Tredgett had come running up from downstairs in a panic. The vibrations from my practice pad could be felt right down to her kitchen; she had no idea what was causing the tremors, but she thought the house would fall down! I showed her the tiny pad and the relief on her face was hilarious; after that I popped a towel under the pad before I started to beat away.

Although the flat was near the tube station, I had to walk along a lengthy subway to reach it. My parents were horrified when they saw this, even though I pointed out that I always carried a pair of hard xylophone sticks in my hand to deter the tramps and drunks who were usually to be found in the subway. 'But what if someone crept up behind you, Evelyn? However would you know they were there?'

The situation was not ideal, but fortunately Ann Rachlin was able to step in yet again with a solution. Her daughter Jan had recently left her flat in Savernake Road near Hampstead Heath. The flat was big enough for four people to share, and the Rachlins suggested that I move in there after Christmas. Liz came with me, and we were joined by Tom, an oboist from the Academy, and Tim, a computer operator, whom we selected from a number of candidates. The flat was super with a large living room that Liz also used as a bedroom, and the rest of us had a bedroom each. Mine was the largest, a blue and white attic room with lots of cupboards and a huge window looking out over the street. Ann had the place repainted so everything was fresh and clean, and she would drop round from time to time to make sure everything was working well. Luckily she always warned us beforehand so we could scurry round for a quick springclean.

The flat was in easy reach of the Academy; equally important, it was minutes away from the lovely walks around Parliament Hill and across Hampstead Heath, with local food shops that stayed open to all hours. I loved it and stayed there for three years, until December 1986; Tim and Tom remained throughout that period, although Liz eventually left, to be replaced by Alison, a trainee accountant. We all got on fine together, mainly leading independent lives, although I saw a lot of Tim. We would treat ourselves to a pizza or an Indian meal as a reward for a hard day's work, and he was terrific about driving me and my equipment around the country as my musical engagements increased. There was never any problem with my practising; I used to put towels over the drums and thud to my heart's content. The only difficulty was in summer when I had the windows open; the people in the flats below would sometimes ask me to calm down a bit, and once, apparently, an irate passer-by shouted 'Shut up' at my windows. Luckily I couldn't hear him.

My drumkit was a gift from the Norman Educational Foundation. One day I received a charming letter from a Mr Findlay Graham of the Foundation, saying I must write if I needed any help during my studies. Always sensitive to any suggestion that I might not be able to manage on my own, I wrote back to say that I was coping fine but thanked him for his concern. I soon received a second letter saying that he was offering to help not because of my deafness, but because he thought that being a percussionist I might need help with purchasing instruments of my own. If so, what would I like most? The Foundation would do their best to obtain what I needed. At first I couldn't quite believe my eyes; it sounded too incredible to be true. However, I quickly wrote back to say that of course equipment was crucial and that I would love to have a snare drum. Why not a drumkit too, wrote Mr Graham. I was simply to choose what I wanted and they would buy it for me. Early in the new year a new Premier Black Shadow seven-piece kit was delivered at Savernake Road.

During my second autumn at the Academy, television suddenly began to feature strongly in my life. I was invited to give an interview on TV AM, and both DR and I appeared to talk and play together. Soon after I had my first meeting with Terry O'Reilly from the BBC. He wanted to make a documentary about me, one of a series of six called *A Will To Win*. I was cautious at our first meeting as I knew that there was a danger that

Terry might take advantage of me and focus on what *he* wanted to say and thought would be good for the camera, rather than showing my point of view. Luckily I took to him immediately; he was completely sensitive to how I wanted to present myself, and to my situation at the Academy. He explained that the aim of the series was to show six different people who were on their way to fulfilling their goal in life. The idea appealed to me greatly and, despite the time I could see that it was going to take out of my studies, I felt right about agreeing to go ahead.

For the following four weeks, Terry became my shadow. We spent hours strolling in Regent's Park, talking about my life and my hopes and ambitions for myself. I felt the film would give me a superb opportunity to say to my teachers and the public, 'Let me have a try at being a soloist. If it doesn't work, fine. All I want is the opportunity to have a go.' Terry really tried to get inside my head and I admired his commitment; I also loved our walks when we would jabber away until it got too dark for me to see, then off we'd go for a meal and more talk.

He was eager to find out what life at the Academy was like for me, and received very full cooperation from the staff. Their only requirement was that Terry's research and the filming should not in any way disrupt classes or the work of staff, my fellow students or myself. Our first sessions took place in October with the BBC crew following me for two days through my schedule: classes, choral conducting, and a session in the library, and Nick, DR and Graeme were interviewed by the late Harold Williamson. My work with Terry and the crew was still continuing the following summer; they filmed me in as many situations as they thought would show the viewers what my life was like and how I was working towards my ambition. The only event they missed was a major prize I won in the summer of

1984, and I don't think Terry will ever forgive me for that!

However, he was able to film my performance at the reception following the Beethoven Fund concert at the Royal Festival Hall in November. On this occasion Sir Georg Solti conducted the London Philharmonic Orchestra. Later, accompanied by Ezra, I played for an audience that included the Duchess of Gloucester, Sir Georg and Lady Solti, the Japanese pianist Mitsuko Uchida and a host of titled, wealthy and talented guests. I wore the purple satin dress made by Mrs Cadger, although looking back I have to confess that it now doesn't appeal at all.

Sir Georg was interviewed for the documentary and said he was sure that I had a future. 'She's such a musical girl, such a natural musician.' Mitsuko Uchida was equally positive. This was all music to my ears (!), of course, but I was particularly pleased and amused to see my mother, normally so down-to-earth about my prospects, throwing caution to the wind and expressing her own hopes for my glorious career, under the influence of all the excitement. Little did I think at that heady moment that in less than four years time I would be working side by side with Sir Georg, playing and recording one of the world's great works for percussion, the Hungarian composer Béla Bartók's Sonata for Two Pianos and Percussion.

The next day saw a more modest but still significant event, a performance at a lunch time concert in the concert room at the Academy. It was the first time that a percussionist had played a solo at the lunch time series, and my first opportunity to perform with Scott Mitchell, a talented young pianist in the same year at the Academy. The performance went so well that we continued to work together for many months at recitals all over the country, until Scott finally decided to concentrate on his own musical development.

Before playing at the lunch time series, every musician

had to have a platform rehearsal, which included tuition on how to walk on and off the stage, general presentation and bowing techniques. I privately thought it rather strange to be given tuition in how to bow, where to fix my eyes in the audience while I was doing it, and even in how often I was allowed to smile. 'For heaven's sake, I'm not a robot!' I kept my thoughts to myself, put the tuition out of my mind and decided to do what I always did in front of an audience, let my response flow naturally.

The small hall was packed, and we received an absolute ovation. Afterwards people complimented me on the openness, honesty and conviction of my playing; they felt that I had communicated something of myself that was quite individual. This reinforced my conviction that what was right for me was to try to express my own feelings to people in my music, instead of worrying about other people's interpretations. Although only one of my fellow percussionists attended the concert, his quiet accolade was worth a million words. 'You should concentrate on solo playing. This looks right for you.' Philip Ellis was an outstanding student and conductor, a musician's musician, with a broad knowledge of repertoire, and a keen eye and ear for the quality of performance. 'Thank you, Philip,' I said, and I really meant it.

Far from offering the gloomy scenario of Orwell's novel, 1984 turned out to be a great year for me. In February there was a repeat on Radio 4 of the *Music on Deaf Ears* interview that I had recorded the previous year with the late Donny B. McLeod; and an invitation to do a week's solo spot in the entertainment *A Drop of Scotch* at HM Theatre, Aberdeen. During the same month I appeared in the *Night of 200 Stars* show in Blackpool which aimed to raise funds for audiology clinics in the area, and recorded my first *Highway* programme with Sir Harry Secombe at Crathie church in Royal Deeside.

The invitation to appear on *Highway* appeared in my pigeonhole at the Academy quite out of the blue. I had of course heard of the series, which is screened on ITV networks on Sundays almost throughout the year. Hosted by Sir Harry, the programme travels throughout the British Isles, and provides an attractive mixture of interviews and entertainment with a 'Sunday' flavour. One of the aims of the programme is to turn the spotlight on people in the community who are remarkable in some way, perhaps for personal courage or their care for others. Ronnie Cass, the programme associate, calls this the 'heart' interview. I was overwhelmed at being invited to appear and tremendously excited at the thought of meeting Sir Harry who seemed himself a man with a quite enormous heart – and a big personality to match. In fact when the time came, straight after my Blackpool performance, I was so excited that I somehow managed to catch a train to Glasgow instead of Edinburgh, but all was well and I finally made it to Royal Deeside in good time. The programme was produced and directed by Martin Cairns from Grampian Television, whom I had met when doing the Dougie Donnelly show. Martin and the programme researcher had apparently suggested my name to Sir Harry.

The pretty village of Crathie is very near Balmoral and the royal family worship at the kirk when they are in residence. I have been to the area before and enjoyed a brief walk around, catching glimpses of quite glorious scenery – mountains and streams with a touch of snow still lying in the hollows, the fields vivid with emerald grass, and the air so fresh and pure that it did me good just to breathe it. Sadly there was not much time for sightseeing; I was only there for one night and spent most of the afternoon being made up and having a wee practice on the piano. Sir Harry likes his interviews to be spontaneous, but this didn't present problems. He was so friendly and easy that I felt completely relaxed.

I played Wishing and then Sir Harry asked me about my life and ambitions.

I remember telling him that as well as being a solo percussionist, I should like one day to teach piano and percussion to deaf as well as hearing children: 'Deaf children just don't get a chance.' I still feel very strongly that deaf children should be introduced to music as early and as much as possible. It's just crazy the way they are so often taken out of contact with normally hearing children and their activities, and shut up in special institutions with no access to the musical experiences that could give them so much pleasure and help them with their speech. Ann Rachlin's work has done a great deal to help teachers become aware of the possibilities; I just wish every deaf child could automatically be put in touch with music as soon as the problem is identified.

I eventually appeared three times that year on *Highway*, following my debut at Crathie kirk with a performance at Inverness with the Scottish National Orchestra of Monti's *Czardas*, arranged for solo percussion and orchestra. The brilliant orchestration was by one of Britain's top arrangers, Peter Knight. On the *Highway Christmas Special* at the end of the year, I turned up as six Evelyns simultaneously playing a percussion ensemble arrangement of Winter Wonderland. We had great fun recording this. Each of the musical parts was filmed separately, of course, and I had to make sure my timing was absolutely accurate so that when they were superimposed the Evelyns didn't finish at different times.

The fan mail and reviews after the first show were terrific, enough to turn anyone's head! I read with enthusiasm about the 'modest and richly talented Evelyn Glennie', my 'rare musical talent', and one person wrote 'I shall never complain about trivial things in life again . . . What a wonderful lass.' Was my head bigger? I certainly hope not. I just felt delighted to have given so much pleasure.

As a result of *Highway*, Ronnie Cass decided that he would like to put some session work my way. The music for the programme was generally pre-recorded by a group of musicians in a London studio, so that Sir Harry, for instance, would mime his songs to a recording when he was filming on location. Session work is demanding – you have to be able to play almost anything on sight, and there is very little rehearsal time; but it is also extremely well-paid and I jumped at the opportunity.

Ronnie's own background was as a pianist and composer. He wrote words and music for the intimate reviews that were popular in London in the fifties and sixties, shows like *For Adults Only* and *The Lord Chamberlain Regrets* that combined topical humour with songs, dancing and sketches. He is tremendously knowledgeable about the great musical shows of the past, and has an outstanding collection of records and tapes which he is still trying to catalogue. One of the high times of his career was when with Peter Myers he wrote the screenplay and score of the film *The Young Ones* and *Summer Holiday*, receiving the coveted Ivor Novello award for the latter. He is a brilliant and virtuoso pianist, and continues to write songs and music for *Highway* where, apart from looking after all the music for the series, he provides many of the words for Sir Harry. Over the years he has become a great friend and helper. The introduction to session work was characteristic of his kindness; not only was I glad of the money, it gave me an opportunity to try out a valuable new experience, and to mix with other musicians, as well as having the fun of meeting some of the stars who joined Sir Harry on the programme.

My first session took place in the middle of July, and I turned up at the studio full of curiosity about what would happen. I discovered that the different sections of the orchestra are recorded on separate tracks and then mixed together afterwards to create the best effect; because of this the sections are split off into compartments around the studio. As the sole percussionist, I found myself in a large booth all to myself, for once able to play the xylophone, timpani and vibraphone to full effect without worrying whether I was going to annoy anybody. The orchestra, conducted by Ted Brennan, another *Highway* regular, played well, and after the session, Alan Franks, the music contractor for the series, took my address so that he could book me for future sessions. According to Ronnie, this meant that I had definitely 'arrived'.

The great event of the summer was the Shell/London Symphony Orchestra Music Scholarship at the beginning of July. So casual was I about this that I never even mentioned to Terry O'Reilly that I had entered for it, so he had no opportunity to film the proceedings. I simply didn't think I had a chance. As it turned out, I was relieved that I hadn't made any fuss about it. I had enough on my plate without having television cameras tracking my every move.

The competition was sponsored by Shell in conjunction with the London Symphony Orchestra with the aim of selecting the winner of an annual music scholarship. Each year the event concentrates on one section of the orchestra, and this year it happened to be timpani and percussion. The judging took place through a series of workshops that would last for a week, with some of the forty-four contestants being weeded out at each stage, although the eliminated contestants were free to continue to attend the workshops if they wished. The preliminary rounds were held at the Henry Wood Hall in Trinity Church Square in London, with two pianos acting as accompaniment as necessary. The final would be staged on the Sunday at the Barbican Centre, when the six finalists would play Andrzej Panufnik's Concertino for Timpani, Percussion and Strings in public with

the London Symphony Orchestra. The prize was prestigious: a gold medal and the princely sum of £3000.

My diary for the week may indicate my fluctuating
progress:

Sunday The preliminary round for the Shell
scholarship took place today at Henry Wood Hall.
There are 44 percussionists taking part. Had my
audition with 2 others. So annoyed with the way
I played – it really was diabolical. I'm praying I
get asked to play during the week.

Monday First workshop day. *Very* very interesting. Players from the LSO gave talks. They cut the
number from 44 to 20, so thank God I was one
of the 20. Had to play xylophone and vibraphone.
Long day. Praying I get to play in next stage.

Tuesday Had to play Beethoven on timps (went
fine) and a wee solo on xylophone. I think it was
a good day for me. It's like having a whole year's
worth of lessons in one day.

Wednesday We were all assessed on timps today
– *Rosenkavalier* and *Rite of Spring*. Played not too
badly. So tired at night. Exactly halfway through.

Thursday Played so badly. I've got through to
the semi-final (13 of us). Hope I play better
tomorrow.

Friday Thought that the panel had forgotten
about me. Had to play the Panufnik Concerto all
day – I was the only one who managed to get
from one end to the other without breaking down.
However, the panel took so long to discuss it.

Saturday I've got through to the final of the

Shell/LSO competition. Very pleased. Six finalists.
Panufnik himself conducted his Concerto. I don't
think he liked my interpretation of it!

I was through to the final stage, and arrived at the
Barbican on the Sunday morning with mixed feelings –
joy to have got so far, and terror that I might now fail
what had become tremendously important to me. For
the final competition the six finalists were divided into
three pairs; one in each pair played percussion, the
other timpani, and we all played the same programme,
of which the major work was Panufnik's Concertino,
commissioned by Shell/LSO for the Scholarship in 1980
and conducted by the composer himself.

I had been drawn to play in the last pair, so had to
wait while the others performed, followed by a short
interval. Then it was our turn. I was playing percussion
and my partner Christopher Thomas, who was also
from the Academy, was playing timpani. Chris was a
very musical player, and I felt happy that we would be
able to coordinate our pieces well together.

Suddenly it was all over. The panel of judges went
away to confer, the audience sat waiting for the decision
and in the meantime arguing about who they thought
should win. Unknown to me, Ronnie Cass had brought
his wife and friends to watch the final, and they were
hotly debating whether one of the players or I had been
better. The contestants were sitting back stage, nobody
talking much; it was far too tense a moment for that.
Then we all had to go back to sit on stage and wait
while the panel read out their verdict.

Third prize went to Derek Gleeson, a student from the
Royal Academy of Music, who won a bronze medal.

The second prize went to Christopher Thomas, also
from the Royal Academy, who won a silver medal.

By this time a small voice was saying inside my head, 'Och well; it was a nice experience anyway,' and I didn't even look when the third name was read out. Then a hand shot out in front of me: 'Well done!' and I thought, 'What, me?' and suddenly it was all happening, the presentation of my gold medal and the cheque, and a riot of hugs and handshakes and congratulations. Evelyn Glennie had won the Shell/LSO Percussion Scholarship for 1984.

My parents hadn't come down to the event because I had not thought it worth mentioning to them, but someone offered to ring them for me and the great news was communicated. It all passed over Mum's head. She was much more interested in when I was coming home for the summer holidays. I felt rather the same myself. It was so unbelieveable that I just couldn't take it in. Later, of course, when they realized what it was all about, Mum and Dad were thrilled, and sad not to have been there.

After all the excitement and interviews with radio and the papers, I settled back into the end-of-term routine. I didn't forget the competition, of course, but it fell into perspective against all the other things I had to do: classes, rehearsals for the orchestra, lessons from Kurt-Hans Goedicke, the LSO timpanist, who gave me a lot of extra help at this time, and the welter of packing up for the summer. About ten days later, a Telemessage arrived. It read:

I WAS THRILLED TO HEAR THE WON-DERFUL NEWS OF YOUR SPECTACU-LAR SUCCESS IN WINNING THE GOLD MEDAL AND FIRST PRIZE IN THE PER-CUSSION COMPETITION. THIS BRINGS YOU MY WARMEST CONGRATU-LATIONS AND EVERY BEST WISH FOR CONTINUED SUCCESS IN THE YEARS AHEAD.
CHARLES.

⊤ Telemessage

KEC4754 LHW2722 PCH0031 P27 BUCK52   18 JUL 1984/710

                                                    Buckingham Palace
                                                    London
                                                    SW1

                                                    18 July 1984

TELEMESSAGE
MISS EVELYN GLENNIE
FLAT C,
82 SAVERNAKE ROAD
LONDON
NW3 2JR

    I WAS THRILLED TO HEAR THE WONDERFUL NEWS OF YOUR SPECTACULAR
SUCCESS IN WINNING THE GOLD MEDAL AND FIRST PRIZE IN THE PERCUSSION
COMPETITION. THIS BRINGS YOU MY WARMEST CONGRATULATIONS AND EVERY
BEST WISH FOR CONTINUED SUCCESS IN THE YEARS AHEAD.

    CHARLES

'Charles?' I mused. 'Whoever could that be?' I laid it to one side and thought no more of it. Later I remembered and showed it to Liz to see if she could think who it was. If I hadn't been deaf, I expect I would have been able to hear her screech three houses away. 'EVELYN!!! Do you know who this is?' She was speechless with excitement and kept waving the sheet at me. At the top of the page I read: 'Buckingham Palace, London, SW1'. Prince Charles had sent me a Telemessage and I hadn't even realized. We laughed and laughed, but I felt so very proud.

In September I went to Glasgow and Aberdeen for a

formal presentation of the award. I still had a year to go at the Academy, but somehow the path ahead seemed clearer. I was finally sure of my destiny at the end of the long haul. First, however, I had to graduate.

16

I graduate with honour

'You must have the score in your head, not
your head in the score.'

Hans von Bülow

My final year flew past in a whirl of activity: classes,
rehearsals, performances, and practice, practice and yet
more practice. I had long had an ambition to graduate
while still a teenager and it now seemed likely that I
would finish at the Academy the following July, when
I was still not yet 20. Although some students feel the
need to prolong their studies beyond three years, I was
eager to test myself in the real world of professional
music, and was straining every nerve to prepare myself
for this great adventure.

My deafness meant extra work for me as the pressure
towards the final examinations mounted. As teachers
began to cram more and more information into classes,
I was having to do a considerable amount of private
study to make sure I was fully informed on the theoretical part of the course, and there was the additional
strain of having to learn all my musical parts off by
heart visually, rather than being able to rely on aural
memory. However, I remained cheerful, encouraged by
the new friends and contacts I was making outside the
Academy, and the increasing opportunities to make an
income for myself.

I was also beginning to take positive steps towards
planning my future. Through my contact with col-

leagues already well established in the music world, I realized that a key figure in the life of any professional musician is his or her manager, whose role is to help the musician to secure engagements, and to look after the publicity and promotional aspect of things. A good manager can have a major influence on her client's career, advising on image, the kind of work to accept and pursue, and helping to build the career profile. At this stage, I was barely aware of needing this kind of help, but I did know how hard it was for a novice to attract any of the more important personalities in the management business. Late that autumn, however, Ann Rachlin introduced me to Nina Kaye of Kaye Artists Management who were based in Chelsea.

Nina's clients included Julian Lloyd Webber, the violinist Anne-Sophie Mutter, and the Israeli piano duo Bracha Eden and Alexander Tamir. I was impressed by Nina's forceful personality and sincere concern for the artists she represented, and made tentative enquiries about the agency. The following May, Nina invited me to lunch and told me she would like to look after me when I left the Academy. At this stage she was advising me to gain experience with a major orchestra before attempting to go solo, and I was both delighted by her interest in me and eager to give serious thought to the opinions of someone with so much experience of the profession. The next day she took me to a concert to watch Eden and Tamir perform, and hinted that I might team up with them when they returned to the UK the following year. It was a wonderful evening, made specially memorable when the Israeli ambassador kissed my hand – my first experience of this courtesy and one that I thoroughly enjoyed.

These kinds of contact gave me food for thought, and in the meantime I continued to work with amateur groups and orchestras outside the Academy, as well as appearing on the Christmas *Highway* and becoming a regular sessions player for the series. Early in the New

Year, Terry O'Reilly's fifty-minute documentary about me, *A Will to Win*, was finally screened on BBC2, prefaced by a major feature about the programme in the *Radio Times*.

The response to the programme was heartening. Friends rushed to congratulate me and my teachers at the Academy were delighted with Terry's sensitive portrayal. As well as the appreciative mail that crammed my pigeonhole over the next few weeks and kept me busy writing back my thanks, viewers' letters were published in the *Radio Times*. One of them interestingly raised the question of parental attitudes to disability; the viewer felt that my case proved that an 'imperfect' child has just as much chance of turning out well as a 'normal' one, given the right kind of parental affection and support. Another viewer commented on my 'superbly well-balanced temperament'. I smiled at this, remembering some of my secret rages in orchestral rehearsals, but it is true that very little bothers me for long. 'Tomorrow is another day' has always been my philosophy and rarely lets me down, but there is no doubt that public support at this time helped tremendously. 'People's enthusiasm and encouragement really do keep me going,' I wrote in my diary. 'It's too late for me to turn back or give up. People expect me to do well and all I can do is to keep climbing – I'll get to where I want to go.'

Another major support was my belief in God, I have never talked about this very much with friends or family, but it has been a force that has quietly sustained me through a number of ups and downs. This feeling that God is with me, a friend who I can talk to in private moments, began quite by chance when I was in my first year at Ellon Academy.

One morning assembly, all the pupils in my class were given a tiny New Testament. I found it very interesting and was puzzled to know why I enjoyed reading the Bible when I found church so dull. I decided that what I hated was being preached at in what I called 'highfaluting' language. It meant nothing to me, I had no sense of communication, and also found the whole business of attending church physically uncomfortable: travelling miles to sit on hard benches in a cold place, in order to be thoroughly bored. I decided this wasn't for me and stopped attending church regularly; instead I read my New Testament when I felt like it, which was usually just before I went to bed. I would underline the words or passages that expressed something to me and began to discover their meaning for myself. I read straight through from cover to cover, and a year or so later I read it all through again and found it meant even more. I could understand what was being said and was able to relate it to what I was doing in my own life. It led me to create my own ideas about how I wanted to live, and those are what I follow now; I haven't been into a church since I came to London.

My belief in God is entirely personal; I've never wanted to influence other people. I still find reading the New Testament a huge inspiration when things aren't going as well as I would like. Rather than talking through problems with friends, I can turn to my Bible and read again the words that I find particularly helpful. It's very peaceful and gives me a feeling of being supported; I never feel lonely even when I'm travelling or having to cope with things on my own. I just feel God is with me and I can talk to Him. This doesn't mean that I accept everything the Bible suggests; I'm still groping around, trying to find out what I think about things. I have no idea, for instance, whether or not there is an afterlife or whether we just go to sleep and disintegrate. It's all a mystery.

My life at this time was very busy, with so many demands being made on me, and my quiet times reading and thinking were very important to my ability to hold on to all the separate threads. Since that time, of course, life has continued to be a flurry of activity, with new people, places, events, and demands being made on me. I continue to talk to God, and have found new sources of inspiration, particularly in two books by Dan Millman, *The Way of the Peaceful Warrior* and *The Warrior Athlete*. They relate very closely to something in me that is difficult to describe, but which I want to preserve. I think it's the quality of spontaneity that children have. They feel no embarrassment, for example, in coming up close to me and really mouthing their words so that I can follow them easily. If children want my attention, they tap me on the arm with no sense of awkwardness, whereas adults will waste time wondering how to make contact. I really value this straightforward approach, ignoring difficulties in order to get what you want out of life, and I try hard to achieve the inner balance that allows me to be direct without fear or caution.

Another source of inspiration at this time was the opportunity to work on Béla Bartók's Sonata for Two Pianos and Percussion. During the reception following the finals for the Shell/LSO Scholarship competition, I had met two young American pianists, Ralph Markham and Kenneth Broadway. They were enthusiastic about the idea of a joint performance of the work, and it was arranged that we would play it early the following February at Farnham and Bourne Music Club at Farnham Maltings. They left it to me to select the timpanist and the obvious choice was Chris Thomas, who had just won second place in the Shell/LSO event.

Over the next months I studied the work closely, following what is still my routine with an unfamiliar work of spending at least a week just looking at the score before I touch an instrument. The piece was first performed early in 1938 with Bartók and his second wife Ditta as pianists, and is generally acknowledged to be a masterpiece. The score includes parts for the two pianos, three timpani, a xylophone, two snare drums (one without snares), clash cymbals, suspended cymbals, bass drum, triangle and tam-tam. Apparently

Bartók felt that the two pianos were necessary to balance the 'frequently very sharp sounds of the percussion'.

In the library, on buses and tubes, I studied the score, working out the structure of the piece, my sticking for the various instruments, whether the parts were solo or accompanied so that I could adjust the level to play at, and so on, marking my findings in pencil on the score. One of Bartók's preoccupations was the balance between the instruments, so that although the percussion is sometimes used simply to illustrate or elaborate on themes introduced by the pianos, it also acts as counterpoint to the piano or even carries main themes. The synchronization between the instruments is crucial, and Bartók gave precise instructions on how the parts should be played, even indicating at times exactly where on the instrument the sound should be made. For instance, the very first note on the cymbal has to be struck on the actual dome, right in the centre, with the heavy end of a drumstick so that it gives a particular kind of very sharp sound. The next note has to be struck on the edge of the cymbal, which gives a warmer sound. This kind of precision in playing was a tremendous challenge and I studied for hours to ensure that I was using the instruments exactly as Bartók had intended.

As this was our first performance together, we needed plenty of time to practise as an ensemble. Inevitably, but to my mind outrageously, we experienced enormous difficulties in finding appropriate venues. We asked permission to practise at the Academy and planned to start first thing in the morning. This alienated the porters because of the 'not before 9 am' rule and on one occasion they tried to move the pianos while Ralph and Ken were playing, on the excuse that they were needed elsewhere.

The rehearsals were scary but exciting. Ralph had never performed the piece and Ken only once, years previously. We had so much to learn. My biggest problem was how to arrange the instruments so that I could see what the pianists were doing as well as being aware of Chris on the timpani – and play my own parts. This had to be fitted in with Bartók's explicit instructions on positioning in order to achieve the balance of sound he wanted. I tried out several positions before I began to feel secure, although I didn't come up with an ideal plan and continued to experiment in subsequent performances. I learnt the piano and timpani scores as well as my own, and always read from the full score, so that I could pick up movement clues from my partners, and took most of my cues from Ken, taking care that I could see his keyboard and the inside of his piano. Now I can almost play the piece from memory, and no longer have these difficulties.

As we grew familiar with the music and one another, we relaxed and were able to use the little time we had to share ideas about how to make the most of the music. It is essential to feel comfortable with one's fellow players in a piece like this; it makes so many demands both on the individual player and on the musicians' ability to work together as a team.

On the day of the performance we arrived early to have the opportunity to rehearse with the instruments provided and to test out the acoustics of the Great Hall at Farnham Maltings. The rehearsal was a disaster. The Bergerault xylophone that had been hired for me was totally unusable; the bars in the top two octaves failed to produce a single note when struck – quite extraordinary! I tried to hire another, but nobody was able to supply one in time. In the end we heard of a man in Farnham who had a xylophone. When it arrived, it turned out to be another Bergerault. I hastily tried out the top two octaves, only to find similar problems. Close your eyes, kind xylophonist from Farnham Maltings; I have to confess that Ken, as an experienced percussionist, shaved and filed several of the bars so that they were vaguely 'in tune'. I kept telling myself that given the problems we had had, the performance could not turn out to be anything but brilliant.

In fact we were pleased with our efforts; the piece moved and had atmosphere and feeling, and we communicated well with one another and with our audience. We delved further into the music than we had been able to do before, taking risks that heightened the excitement and made the piece explode with freshness. The audience were delighted and we received a terrific review from Peter Sanger, who noted in particular the precision with which we coordinated the parts, and said that we 'kept the audience totally absorbed in the music from mysterious beginning to hushed end', taking them 'into the heart of Bartók's very particular sound world'.

This was only the beginning of my contact with this richly satisfying work, and I am still learning how to make the most of the music if offers. The flavour of the work changes, too, depending on who I play it with. After my performance with Ken and Ralph, James Blades was to give me crucial advice about the xylophone part which helped me to improve my performance. Interestingly I had the opportunity to play the work again in February 1990 with Ralph and Ken, and Martin Gibson on timpani, and it was satisfying to find that our performances had matured.

Soon after this I started to work with a fellow student, Kenneth Dempster, on a piece that he was composing specially for the marimba, vibraphone and orchestra. My xylophone and marimba had been sent down from the farm so that I had more freedom to practise in these crucial months before finals, and Kenneth and I also worked on the piece at the Academy. It was a rather modern piece and Nick Cole, ever an enthusiast for the more classical orchestral pieces, was less than complimentary when he heard me practising in the corridor. '*What* is that?' he enquired, incredulous. I explained. 'Rather you than me.' I was left to my own devices.

The *Concerto Palindromos* was dedicated to me and

we performed it at a lunchtime concert in the Duke's Hall at the Academy, with Kenneth conducting an orchestra that he had managed to put together from interested colleagues. The principal, Sir David Lumsden, was enthusiastic. It was the first percussion concerto that had been played at the Royal Academy of Music and he thanked us for the 'lesson in percussion'. The piece did not become part of my regular repertoire as Kenneth went to the States before completing the revisions he had planned, but it was an enjoyable experiment with new repertoire.

One of the other ways in which I planned to expand my percussion repertoire was by writing to interesting composers to ask them to create a piece specially for me. Looking back on it, I am stunned by my naivety; I could have landed myself in terrible trouble if they had all responded positively – and demanded fat fees for the commission! Luckily, only a few rose to the challenge and they were usually friends and fellow students. However, I did have a terrific response from the Armenian-born composer and conductor, Loris Tjeknavorian. He sent me a parcel of signed scores and a recording of some of his work, with a friendly letter. I was delighted, as his percussion writing is unique and beautiful, as is demonstrated in pieces such as his Symphony No 1, *Requiem for the Massacred*, written in 1974, which makes sustained and imaginative use of twenty-six percussion items, incorporating instruments associated with the Armenian church or Islam – bells, cymbals, trumpet and drums. Sadly, nothing so far has come of this contact, although I hope we will work together in the future.

Although I couldn't learn new pieces by listening to tapes and records, I did spend time hugging the loudspeakers of Tim's stereo system, or sitting with them between my knees, feeling the beat and vibrations of pieces that interested me. Another way of getting in touch with music was to sit with a clattery old portable tape recorder in my lap, one that vibrated as much as possible so I could experience the waves of sound through my body. I still use both these techniques.

I was increasingly anxious to master the four-mallet techniques that were so necessary for the virtuoso playing required by modern compositions. Derek Gleeson, who had come third in the Shell/LSO competition, gave me advice on the Burton grip, developed by the jazz vibraphonist Gary Burton in the 1960s. This offers considerably more power and independence of movement than I had experienced with the traditional crossed-stick grip that is normally used by orchestral players. However, I was not to perfect the Burton method until I studied in Switzerland some time later. In the meantime, I wrote to Keiko Abe to ask her if she could give me some lessons on the marimba. Keiko uses the traditional grip, so I hoped that she could help me sort out some of my problems with this; but my main motive was to benefit from her virtuosity and musicianship. Interestingly, when I did finally get together with Keiko, we spent no time at all on mallet work. What was essential to her was the study and interpretation of meaning in a work, and through her I developed my sense of curiosity about the composer's intentions and my sensitivity to how these were expressed.

All this was in the future; I didn't hear from Keiko and, finally, hearing that she was performing in Berlin that June, I decided I would go there and try to speak to her in person. Tim obligingly agreed to accompany me and we set off from Gatwick at 5 pm on 6 June, arriving at the School of Music in Berlin just in time for Keiko's concert at 8 pm. It was a marvellous evening. After the recital, I managed to speak to Keiko who couldn't have been more friendly and helpful. We agreed to meet the next day.

Naturally, we hadn't troubled to book rooms in advance and were rather surprised to learn from some of the students at the concert that there wasn't a spare bed in the town. There was a major flower festival in Berlin, and hotels and hostels were packed with market gardeners. Luckily one of the percussionists who had accompanied Keiko spoke excellent English and, hearing about our plight, invited to stay at his flat for the night. Andreas turned out to be a super person and we had a wonderful late-night pizza together, before settling to sleep on his floor. At least it was better than a park bench, I philosophized next morning, ruefully rubbing my bruises.

The meeting with Keiko went well. She let me play on her five-octave Yamaha marimba ('WOW! It was so gorgeous!' I wrote in my diary), and said she would be delighted to give me lessons, perhaps when she was next in Europe or maybe I could travel to Japan. She also gave me advice on marimba music and where to buy it, and I had some tips on technique from the percussion lecturer at the music college, a charming character named Klaus, who presented me with two pairs of marimba sticks. I came home ecstatic, feeling that London was very dismal compared to the fun I had had in Berlin. However, Tom cheered me up as I walked through the door at Savernake Road. I had passed my piano final. WHOOPEE!!!

It seems rather incredible that my finals were slotted in around the busy events of the spring and early summer of 1985, but exams there were and I do seem to have passed them all. I was also continuing to win awards. In May I auditioned for an Ian Fleming Trust Music Education Award. I had sat the final written harmony paper at the Academy in the morning, before rushing to the Wigmore Hall to play the side drum for the Trust, and then on to Chelsea for a rehearsal of Ravel's *Bolero* with the Chelsea Symphony Orchestra. I felt that even if my audition failed, I could at least say that I had played in the prestigious Wigmore Hall, but I soon heard from the Trust that I had won £1,000 towards the purchase of instruments. With the thought of a possible trip to Japan on the horizon, I became increasingly anxious to gain as much sponsorship as I could over the next year, and this was just one of the trusts and foundations that I applied to for grants and awards to help fund both instruments and travel.

As the examination results became known and we all began to plan for graduation, I heard that I had been awarded the Hilda Deane Anderson Prize for Orchestral Playing; I had also won the James Blades Prize for Percussion (I had won the James Blades Prize for Timpani and the Hugh Fitch Prize for Percussion in 1984). Most exciting of all, Sir David Lumsden awarded me the Queen's Commendation Prize for All-round Excellence, the Academy's top accolade. I was to graduate on 10 July with my GRSM (Graduate of the Royal School of Music) Honours degree; I'd received my LRAM (Licentiate of the Royal Academy of Music) in both piano and percussion in my second year.

My parents came to London for the graduation ceremony on 10 July. Princess Diana presented the prizes, and I had the great honour to be the final student to step on to the platform, to receive the Queen's Commendation award. Later, at the reception for students, staff and relatives in the Duke's Hall, I was presented to the princess, who astonished me by her natural beauty. She was pleasant and interested; although I had to curb my enthusiasm for a wee gossip. You can only speak when you're spoken to when hobnobbing with royalty; no question of asking after Prince Charles or chatting about the royal children!

So much time, so much effort, so many hopes and dreams – and suddenly I was there, home and dry, a graduate of the Royal Academy of Music. Perhaps the moment when I realized this most strongly was not at the ceremony at all, but a few days earlier in David Robinson's office. I had popped in to ask him what he would like as a present from the students who were leaving, and he took the opportunity to say that he would miss me and to wish me well. 'Goodbye to Evelyn Glennie music student; hello to Evelyn Glennie professional musician.' Just having DR say these words gave me an extraordinary sensation – a rush of joy and nostalgia mingled with a faint cold shiver of anticipation. Now I was really on my own; Evelyn Glennie was finally going solo.

17

Going solo

'Music is your own experience, your
thoughts, your wisdom. If you don't live it,
it won't come out of your horn.'

Charlie Parker

I left the Academy with no fixed ideas about how my
career would progress, although I was quite sure what
I wanted to achieve. Anything might happen and I was
prepared for every eventuality, including failure. My
one aim was to make a name for myself as a soloist,
both in recital work and with reputable ensembles and
orchestras, and I was determined to get the best out of
every opportunity that came my way and to do my
uttermost to win through the obstacles. Fortunately, I
already had a number of engagements booked and the
next few months exceeded all my expectations. From
the moment I waved my parents off after graduation
until I fell into bed long after dawn on New Year's Day
1986, there was never a dull moment. The days flew
past full of new faces, places and music to play, and
night after night my diary records, 'Great day', 'Good,
useful day', 'Interesting day, full of surprises'.

Looking back, it isn't at all astonishing that I found
life so enjoyable. I was only just 20, living in an attractive flat in a leafy part of London with pleasant flatma-
tes, and spending all my time exploring work that I
loved, with the freedom to organize my own schedule
and finances. I was also lucky enough to have my man-

ager Nina Kaye to advise me on everything from professional engagements to how I had my hair styled, and good friends in the music world to introduce me to new ideas, repertoire and opportunities to perform. God seemed to be on my side – for that period at least – and I was idyllically happy.

One of my first priorities was to earn enough money to pay for all my expenses. It was not just a question of food and rent. As my engagements increased, so did the need to invest in my own instruments with all the related costs of cases and boxes to transport them to venues both in the UK and overseas. I began my collection of ethnic instruments at this time, looking out for members of the percussion family not commonly used or available in Britain or even America, but items that I wanted to learn to play and to incorporate into my performances. I was building my percussion repertoire and investing huge sums in music, much of it ordered from North America, as well as buying tapes and records. Advised and encouraged by Nina, I was also beginning to take a keen interest in my personal presentation, studying fashion and makeup, and having to spend considerable sums on evening dresses and attractive clothes and hairstyles for performances and media interviews.

All this cost money, but somehow or other I managed, with the help of various grants and awards to buy instruments and to assist me to travel and study abroad. *Highway* sessions continued to be profitable, and increasingly I was being offered the opportunity to earn an income through concerts and recitals. One regular but minor source of revenue during these first months was teaching. After the summer Graeme Humphrey was away on a tour of Australia and New Zealand for several months, and asked me to take his private piano students. This meant a long haul out to Dulwich and Norwood twice a week, and I always regretted the time wasted hanging around on chilly platforms and at bus stops, but I was glad of the money and enjoyed the experience. Whatever my pupils first thought about having a deaf teacher, they very quickly realized that I was there to work and would be prompt to notice if they didn't practise and improve.

Health became a major enthusiasm at this time. Inspired by the energy and power of the Japanese 'Kodo' drummers, who Ann Rachlin took me to see at the Queen Elizabeth Hall, I established a rigorous programme of self-improvement in order to be in peak condition for performing. I would regularly jog round Hampstead Heath for an hour or so at six o'clock in the morning, and did exercises in the cramped space allowed by the growing collection of instruments in my bedroom. I was also strict about my diet, buying up the local fruit and vegetable stall and banning chocolate biscuits, although the benefits of this regime were frequently undermined by the huge pizzas that Tim and I often indulged in!

Eating is one of my joys, and I have many fond memories of hearty and delicious meals enjoyed on my travels, snatched or eaten at leisure in restaurants, cafés and snack bars, in hotel rooms and private homes, daintily served on delicate china or gobbled up out of paper bags. Luckily, weight doesn't seem to be a problem for me; I expend so much energy performing and rushing from engagement to engagement that there is little risk of bursting out of one of my elegant gowns even during a particularly strenuous performance.

I was also working hard to improve my techniques on the range of percussion instruments that I had available. Every spare moment was spent practising, developing strength, flexibility and stamina, and learning new repertoire to try out in the recitals and concerts that I hoped would come my way. I was still concerned to find a way of playing with four mallets that would achieve all the effects that I needed to tackle worthwhile pieces from the marimba literature, but it wasn't until

October that I finally came to terms with the grip that suits me best. The breakthrough couldn't have happened in more beautiful surroundings – in Tenero on the Swiss/Italian border.

My journey to Switzerland was a big adventure. I had arranged to attend a four-day vibraphone and marimba course run by Ruud Wiener and Peter Prommel. Ruud is a respected vibraphone teacher, composer and performer in Europe; Peter is a Dutch percussionist. While the course presented no difficulties, the prospect of travelling by myself to Zürich and then to Tenero was a little daunting. In fact the journey went without a hitch. I flew to Zürich from Heathrow, and went to the railway information office at Zürich airport to enquire how to get to Tenero. English seems to be no problem in Switzerland, so I was soon on the correct train for my destination, where Ruud picked me up. The scenery along the route was breathtaking: ranges of snow-capped mountains with tiny villages on the lower slopes, all sparkling in glorious sunshine.

The course was international with Italian, Dutch and French/Swiss students as well as myself. There were only ten of us, which meant that we had plenty of teacher attention, but I was also able to learn from the other students' techniques and use of repertoire. One girl, a Dutch percussionist studying in Amsterdam, was both good and a workaholic. This immediately inspired me to work even harder myself. 'I'm determined to be as good if not better,' I wrote anxiously in my diary; 'I must be – she can hear – I can't.'

At last, too, I was able to study the different grips for four-mallet work and to decide which would suit me best. We looked at the traditional method, the crossed grip or 'scissors' and at more recent techniques, including the Burton, Musser and Stevens grips. Each of the grips relies on a slightly different way of positioning and gripping the mallets with the fingers; what I wanted was a method that would allow me to regulate the power with which I struck the notes, as well as giving me the flexibility to change the intervals between notes as quickly as I wanted to, and to have dynamic independence, varying the crescendo effects of individual notes, for example, and allowing each mallet independent action.

After some experimentation, it became obvious that I would be happiest with the Burton technique. After being shown how it worked, I was able to develop the grip on my own. It was to open the door to all kinds of new repertoire, enabling me to tackle the Japanese literature, concertos and *études* and many other pieces with new confidence.

I came back from Switzerland delighted with all I had learnt, and sad to leave behind some valuable new friends. At the station Ruud gave me a parcel containing a book on vibraphone solos which he had composed, with a little message: 'For your courage, perseverance and musicianship'. Sweet man; he was a terrific teacher and determined to help each of us to get all we could from the course.

Towards the end of October, I had the opportunity to give my first public performance of the Paul Creston Marimba Concertino. I had been invited to play with the Kent Schools Symphonic Wind Band at the Marlowe Theatre in Canterbury. Our first rehearsal had been somewhat chaotic as we tried to get our bearings with this complex work, which presents a tremendous challenge to a young orchestra, but by the night of the performance the Creston went smoothly, and I followed this in the second half of the programme with lighter pieces including the sparkling *Czardas* with the band, and my own A Little Prayer. I was studying ragtime pieces, as I find them excellent technical material for the xylophone, so I played the Black and White Rag as an encore, and then the band played Land of Hope and Glory, with me joining in on the cymbals, and the audience waving wee Union Jacks, just like the last night of the Proms.

Another young group, the Bromley Schools Boys Choir, invited me to be their guest at their yearly concert in November at the Purcell Room on the South Bank. I had the good fortune to play with the accomplished pianist Philip Smith. To my delight the performance went extremely well and Philip became my regular pianist. Apart from having a terrific sense of humour – and an appetite that far exceeds anything I might be able to muster – Philip is a marvellous partner, working with me with great skill and flexibility so that we get the best out of our performance together.

The great event of that autumn was my trip to North America with James Blades. We had been planning it for months and finally the great day came. On 14 November, I set out for Heathrow and what I hoped would be a turning point in my life. I was going to Los Angeles to the Percussive Arts Society's International Convention, Pasic '85, where I was hoping to have my mind stretched and my horizons expanded by contact with the many mainly American performers and percussion experts who attend this annual conference.

I met James at Heathrow and we sat together talking almost non-stop through the ten-hour journey. We flew over Iceland, Greenland and Canada and I was able to admire the terrific scenes below us of snow on the mountains. We were met at Los Angeles airport by Robert Zildjian the President of Sabian Cymbals, who drove us to the Sheraton Universal Hotel where the convention was being held. I had first encountered Robert at the British Music Fair at Olympia in August 1985, and he has become a good friend since. Sabian cymbals are magnificent instruments, which I was pleased to endorse, and I was thrilled the following November when Robert presented me with several pairs of handmade cymbals for my own use. Our reception at the hotel was heartwarming as everyone recognized

James and came up to greet him. The young people were carrying his monumental *Percussion Instruments and their History*, and clustered round for him to sign their copies.

The next two days were spent in a flurry of workshops and meetings. With over 2000 percussionists milling about, I couldn't fail to make new friends or pick up some useful tips, and I made the best of the opportunity. I was due to give an hour-long solo performance on the third day, but had the usual hassle trying to get hold of instruments that I felt comfortable playing – yes, even at a percussion convention! All the instruments were on display at the various booths, but finally a collection was gathered and I settled down to give what was billed as 'the American concert-premiere' of two movements from the Suite for Timpani by the British composer Graham Whettam. It is a difficult piece, but I acquitted myself reasonably well. 'Snare drumming fine, xylo could have been better, timpani was diabolical' was my own summary of the whole event. James was in his element; he did all the talking, introducing the pieces and sharing a snare drum and timpani duet with me.

One of the interesting aspects of American performers that I became very aware of at the convention was their tendency to focus on technique. Nine times out of ten their discussions would be about how a piece was being played rather than paying attention to the music itself. When I came to the end of A Little Prayer, the audience were absolutely silent for a few seconds and then gave me a standing ovation, many of them in tears – I know that both James and I had tears in our eyes. The audience reacted in this emotional way because for once, in this very simple piece, they had been invited to listen to the silences in the music, and they couldn't find anything to say about technique. What they were experiencing spoke first and foremost to the heart.

Silence in music is very important for me – leaving

space between the phrases without feeling the need to cover it up by lifting a stick, for example, so that the audience is distracted from experiencing the silence by movement. When I perform I consciously use this space in different ways. It's sometimes nice for the audience to have a moment at the beginning or end of a piece to prepare themselves for what is going to come or to reflect on what they have heard before they start to clap or rush on to something else. If a concert finishes in a super-dramatic way I just need a breather to say 'Whooh!' That space is so important.

My recital set the seal on my acceptance at the convention. Billy Cobham, one of the greatest exponents of heavy rock, was there, invited by James to my recital. He had to catch a plane, but as the audience burst into applause, he walked down the aisle to congratulate me, before hurrying off. James was delighted; 'He's a number one act, a world beater,' he kept saying. Other people rushed to chat to me at the end and overwhelmed me with compliments both on my playing, and my ability to communicate and give a genuine performance. One man even wanted to publish A Little Prayer.

The rest of the day was spent meeting yet more people, including Gary Burton the great jazz-vibraphonist, and attending a marvellous banquet in the evening, where I had the honour of sitting at the Sabian table. After the meal and speeches, Gary Burton and Makoto Ozone, a Japanese jazz pianist, gave a wee concert, which was quite brilliant. When I finally fell into bed I was so excited and exhilarated by the day's events that I cried my eyes out. People were so warm and friendly, and I was delighted to be mingling with all these dedicated and talented musicians.

The next morning I took a last look around the exhibition to make sure that I had collected all the catalogues and information that I needed, and to say goodbye to my new friends. James then decided he wanted to go to Disneyland so off we went with Celeste Richards, the wife of Emil Richards, who recorded the percussion sounds for Disneyland. What a place! We met Pinocchio, Pluto, the Seven Dwarfs, Mickey Mouse and Minnie, and a host of other familiar characters. It was like a different world. Finally, we had to go back to the hotel to collect our bags, say another goodbye, this time to Celeste, hop into a limousine (a great thrill) and head for the airport. We were absolutely starving by the time we arrived as we'd had nothing all day except a 'lifesaver', but once on the flight we were able to eat, and James soon fell asleep, exhausted by the day's events. No such luck for me; my seat was wedged in the upright position, so I spent a busy night thinking about all I had experienced and wishing it could have gone on forever. One thing was certain – I was going to be a regular visitor to Pasic from now on.

I returned with a new determination and immediately plunged into a spate of work and writing letters to my new friends in America. Jonathan Bose, who was a percussion teacher at Trinity College of Music, gave me a lesson in Latin percussion: castanets, tambourine and *cabasa*, a pear-shaped gourd which has beads strung around it on a net. As you turn the gourd, the beads rasp against grooves in the side of the gourd producing a high-pitched scraping noise. Jonathan was a terrific teacher and the few hours he was able to spare gave me the basics of Latin rhythms and styles, which I worked on my own to master.

I was also studying French, pressing on despite the fact that I had no idea whether I was pronouncing the words correctly. Language tapes were of no use to me! Perhaps more importantly, I was teaching myself basic phrases in Japanese, ready for my trip to Japan. Keiko had sent me a charming letter after our meeting in Berlin, urging me to come to Japan as her European schedule was so busy. 'It will be a great adventure for you to stay in Japan, but if you have a strong will, it should be a fantastic experience, I believe.' I was determined to go later the following year, and was working to save enough money to spend several weeks in that most expensive of cities, as well as to pay my fees for Keiko's tuition, and travel expenses.

The media continued to take an interest in me. *Reader's Digest* planned to publish the *Radio Times* article which had prefaced *A Will To Win* in their 'Heroes for Today' feature, and I had a long session with their photographer. I still hadn't got used to the idea that it takes at least an hour to arrange the lighting and 'set', and two minutes to take the pictures! The feature appeared the following February and I received the usual spate of warmhearted and supportive letters from readers. The women's magazine *My Weekly* were also planning a feature for February, and I had another photo session and an interview with Valerie Ward. The feature was very well written, but it inevitably concentrated on my deafness rather than my music, and it was about this time that I really began to think about publicity and to determine that my work as a percussionist must be the focus of attention rather than my hearing.

The year ended with the kind of razzmatazz that I like best: a chance to wow an audience with some lively stick work. The BBC invited me to appear on their Hogmanay programme which was being screened live from the Aberdeen studios from late at night on 31 December. This meant a busy shopping session with Delphine Gordon, the BBC wardrobe lady from Glasgow. We found a long heavy cotton dress at Laura Ashley that seemed just right, although when I looked at the price tag I was pleased that the BBC were footing the bill. Over a healthy – and tasty – vegetarian lunch, I took the opportunity to pick Delphine's brains about fashion and suitable colours for appearing on television. The programme was great fun. My stint was just after midnight and I played on a Scottish selection with the fiddle orchestra to a wildly appreciative audience. After a night of hobnobbing with the other guests on the programme and then visiting friends and relatives with Mum, I collapsed into bed at 6 am. Happy 1986, Evelyn!

18

Testing my wings

'Know your stuff, know who you're going
to stuff, then go ahead and stuff them!'
    As told to Jeffrey Vaughan Martin, con-
ductor of the Kent Youth Wind Orchestra

The year began with two rather different but to me
equally important events: the Radio 4 documentary *The
Glennie Determination* and a guest appearance on
Wogan. The musicologist Antony Hopkins compiled
and presented the documentary, which included interviews with David Robinson, Andrzej Panufnik and my
mother. It was well received by reviewers. David Wade
in *The Times* said that the examples of my playing were
'electrifying', and Andrew Grimes in the *Manchester
Evening News* quoted my favourite maxim, 'If you want
to do something, there is nothing in this world that will
stop you doing it. That's for sure.' He also mentioned
my frustration with bearded conductors: 'She . . . has
not yet developed the X-ray vision that would enable
her to read instructions through a thick curtain of hair.'
One very unexpected result of the programme was a
letter and generous cheque from a wellwisher in Devon,
who has continued to be a benefactor. I felt very humble
writing back my thanks. This kind of warm response
from a stranger always makes me want to rush off to
express my pleasure and gratitude in person; paper
seems so inadequate.

Luckily Terry Wogan didn't have a beard, but I suspected he would be tricky to handle in other ways. The invitation came by phone on 9 January; I had just two weeks to prepare. I watched both the programmes in the intervening weeks and took careful note of what happened. In particular I was interested in Terry's interviewing techniques. I anticipated that he would want to focus on my deafness; I was determined to talk about music.

I also went shopping for a new outfit, bearing in mind all I had learnt about suitable colours and presentation for television. In the end I bought a very pretty pink blouse which I wore with a three-quarter-length black skirt and some very expensive and dressy new shoes decorated with tiny glittering beads. I had a private dress rehearsal in my bedroom two days before the event and thought I looked quite stunning – just the thing for *Wogan!* In particular, the skirt had to be wide enough for me to leap about playing the energetic jazzed-up version of the Maple Leaf Rag that I had just been arranging for the xylophone.

On the day, a taxi came to take me to the Shepherd's Bush Theatre. I rehearsed with the pianist, drummer and bass player, who were terrific, and we also did a sound/camera/lighting rehearsal. Terry came into my dressing room at about 6.30 to introduce himself. He was very friendly and relaxed, and I looked forward to our meeting in public. There were a number of other guests, including Jilly Cooper and Elvis Costello, and we all chatted in the greenroom until it was our turn to go on. I was the last guest, to my delight, but the whole performance and interview went so fast that it was over before I knew it had started! I whizzed through Maple Leaf Rag, giving it as much oomph as I could to get the audience going, then Terry and I had a chat in which I managed to do most of the talking, telling him about my ambitions as a percussionist, and about my belief that music comes as much from the heart as through the ears.

There was a tremendous response from viewers to my interview with Terry, apparently the largest ever, and to my surprise the BBC very soon asked me to return for a second programme. However, much as I'd enjoyed it, I decided that it would be best to wait for a while. Nina and my other advisers, including the Rachlins, were concerned that too many appearances on a popular programme would undermine my still fragile status as a serious musician. My own view was more flexible; I didn't worry about becoming 'categorized', I simply felt that it would be a good idea to gather a few more experiences before I talked to Terry again.

Soon after this, a great opportunity was offered, which was to occupy much of my emotional and professional energy over the next few months: my Wigmore Hall debut with a performance of Bartók's Sonata for Two Pianos and Percussion with Bracha Eden and Alexander Tamir. Based in Israel, these two pianists have established a worldwide reputation for their work in expanding the duo piano repertoire. They have given many performances in the Far East, Europe and America, and are particularly celebrated for their work on Brahms. The Bartók was a familiar piece for them and I was delighted and honoured to be invited to share their Wigmore Hall engagement. To my gratification I was to receive equal billing.

As well as works by Stravinsky, Poulenc and Milhaud for the two pianists, the programme was to include Toshiro Mayuzumi's Concertino for Xylophone, in which I was accompanied by Philip Smith on the piano, and the American composer Niel DePonte's Concertino for Marimba, an interesting short piece which displays the instrument well. Mayuzumi is a Japanese composer, innovatory in style, incorporating the characteristic idioms of late Romanticism, with jazz and Oriental themes. The Concertino has a strong Oriental flavour;

it was written in 1965 and is his only solo composition for percussion, although he uses it extensively in other works. Although very different, both works offer opportunities for technical skill and some virtuoso playing and I was pleased to have the chance to demonstrate my capabilities.

The first question was whether there would be room on the Wigmore Hall stage for all the percussion equipment. That and a hundred and one other administrative problems were left to the long-suffering Kaye Artists to sort out, and they worked with dedication on the project. There was also the question of who would play timpani for the Bartók sonata. I first thought of Tristan Fry, who knows the work well and whose musicianship I admire. However, he had always played the piece with James Holland and was reluctant to work with anyone else. I then suggested contacting Nigel Thomas who had won the Shell/LSO award in 1980 and is a highly gifted musician. Although he had never performed the work before, he was willing to try. The first step was for Nigel and myself to meet to talk about the work and for me to pass on any ideas that I had learnt from my performance with Markham and Broadway. We rehearsed at the Royal Academy of Music, meeting early in the mornings but managing to avoid any disputes with the porters, and soon became familiar with playing together.

Nina Kaye had arranged two preliminary performances of our complete Wigmore Hall recital at the Adeline Genee Theatre in East Grinstead on 5 May and the Yehudi Menuhin School on 7 May; the Wigmore Hall date was six days later on 13 May. The four of us met for our first rehearsal on 23 April. I arrived early at the rehearsal room to set up and arrange my instruments. By the time everyone else arrived, I was exhausted, my hands and arms aching with lugging around the heavy equipment. Nigel was in an even worse state; he had left his stick case and music at the Royal Festival Hall the previous evening and they had been stolen. We agreed that I could lend him sticks; his main concern was to get hold of a copy of his part – and quick, before the duo arrived! He zoomed over to the Guildhall School of Music and Drama, walked into the library without any notice being taken of him, found a copy of the Bartók and sauntered out again without a blink of an eyelash from anyone. He arrived just after Eden and Tamir, but they were less shocked by the story of his mishap than by his appearance. He was wearing the then fashionable crewcut with a small pigtail down the back of his neck.

Once we had begun to play together, I forgot about these small misadventures and became absorbed in the business of exchanging ideas on how to perform the work. The aim of the rehearsal was to get to know one another and to smooth out any rough edges in our performance, and as we became more relaxed the ideas flowed, with the pianists receptive to Nigel and my ideas, despite their long experience of the work. Alexander Tamir was particularly struck with the musical effect of the xylophone in certain sections, and I breathed a quiet thank you to James Blades, as his advice had proved crucially helpful in achieving this.

Our next rehearsal was at East Grinstead at the Adeline Genee Theatre just prior to the performance. The acoustics in the hall were rather dry, so we had to compensate for this, and we were also working on interpretation and general musical points. The performance was encouraging. There was room for improvement, but the audience obviously enjoyed it and we felt satisfied. The performance at the Yehudi Menuhin School went even better, with all of us playing with more confidence and daring as a quartet. At the rehearsal beforehand, Alexander Tamir suggested a different interpretation for the opening of the second movement, which he imagined almost as a funeral march, where phrasing and dynamics are so crucial. I tried it out during the evening performance and was interested in the effects, although I found I didn't entirely agree with his view.

The rehearsal for the Wigmore Hall took place on the morning of the performance and was something of a nightmare. We had planned to work from nine o'clock till lunchtime, but most of this time had to be spent laying heavy risers on the platform so that the timpani and percussion could be seen behind the pianos. The performance was to be recorded by Radio 3, which turned out to be a blessing as, in the absence of any stagehands, the performers and the radio crew had to perform this labour. In the meantime, I was scurrying round trying to organize a quick delivery of the bass drum that the hire firm had forgotten. The stage is so tiny that it took ages to fit the timpani and percussion on to the space available, and finally we had to accept that there was no way we could fit the bass drum and four timpani on stage simultaneously. Nigel courageously volunteered the loss of one of his timpani. All we had time for at the rehearsal was to run the piece from beginning to end to amend any balance problems.

I spent the afternoon auditioning for the Henry and Lily Davis Fund, and later heard that I had been awarded £750, which was a great bonus for my trip to Japan. A pause for a cup of tea with Mum, who was in London for the occasion, and then I set off again – my Wigmore Hall debut was about to begin. We played the Bartók before the interval and received a tremendous reception. I played from my heart, giving every ounce of emotional and technical energy, and was pleased with the result. Bracha was concerned that sections had been too loud, but Alexander and Nigel were well satisfied.

So, it appears, were the critics. Stephen Pettitt in *The Times* commented on my professionalism and control in the Bartók, and was impressed by my virtuosity and capabilities in both the DePonte and the Mayuzumi.

EDEN & TAMIR
Duo Pianists

EVELYN GLENNIE
Percussion

With Nigel Thomas (timpani) and Philip Smith (piano)
Tuesday 13th May 1986 7.30pm
Wigmore Hall

Box Office 01 935 2141 Tickets £5.50 £4.50 £3.50 £2.50

Stravinsky	Five Easy Pieces
Milhaud	Scaramouche
Mayuzumi	Concertino for Xylophone and piano
DePonte	Concertino for Marimba
Poulenc	Sonata for two pianos
Bartok	Sonata for two pianos and percussion

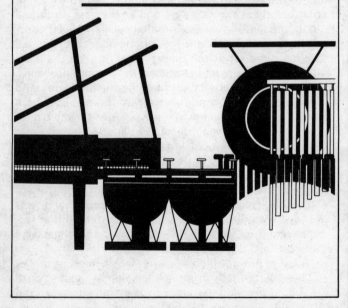

Interestingly – and flatteringly – he devoted most of his review to my performances, and focused on what continues to be a source of difficulty for the professional reviewer, 'the lack of very much solo percussion music of any real quality' apart from the kinds of work that he suggested are so avant-garde that audiences tend to flee from them. Geoffrey Norris, writing in *The Daily Telegraph*, saw the DePonte and Mayuzumi works as 'unashamed showpieces', but was happy to sit back, and 'marvel at the sheer artistry [Miss Glennie] brought to it'. He felt I brought to the concert 'a degree of musical and technical accomplishment which was never short of breathtaking'.

My next major engagement was a performance with the Scottish National Orchestra of Alexander Lepak's Concerto for Mallet Instruments. Funnily enough, this too was preceded a few days earlier by an audition for another award, this time from the Countess of Munster Musical Trust. My success with this meant that my trip to Japan in the autumn was now assured. I travelled to Glasgow in a great mood, looking forward to seeing old friends in the SNO. The concert was to be held in the Scottish Exhibition Centre and was my first concerto with a professional orchestra, as well as the first UK performance of the Lepak. Alexander Lepak is an American composer and conductor, and himself a timpanist and percussion player. The concerto is a virtuoso piece, using vibraphone, marimba, xylophone and chimes, and featuring jazz themes as well as quieter and more plaintive melodies. The work requires considerable technique and musicality, and I had been studying it for several months.

To my consternation, the first rehearsal with Bryden Thomson and the orchestra at the SNO centre was depressing. I found it difficult to get used to having an orchestra behind me, and the acoustics meant that I was feeling several different tempos simultaneously and losing my balance and coordination. I was devastated, but recognized that part of the problem was getting used to the way in which a professional orchestra rehearses, and I managed not to lie awake all night worrying about it. Thankfully the rehearsal next morning in the concert hall went well, and by evening I felt on top form and relieved that yet another 'first' had been successfully negotiated.

Fortunately another good review boosted my morale; writing in the *Glasgow Herald*, Kenneth Walton said that I possessed 'a skill and musicality to rival any'. He seemed to think that this made up for any shortcomings in the Lepak, but all this negative criticism about repertoire made me resolve to renew my efforts to find works that combined music of a high quality with the opportunity for demonstrating technical virtuosity. Somewhat despairingly I wrote in my diary, 'I don't know what I can do to solve the problem. I could never write anything better myself so I must perform the music that's there.' These days, I see the matter in less gloomy terms than the critics, and am continuing to extend my repertoire both with specially commissioned works by modern composers, and by incorporating a range of music in my programmes, from adaptations of the classical to Latin, rags, blues and so on.

The prospect of more trips abroad had been hovering enticingly on my horizon for some months, and suddenly I was off again, bound for Queensland, Australia with the Grampian Schools Percussion Ensemble, this time as guest soloist. I spent the journey reading Antony Hopkins' autobiography; working with him on *The Glennie Determination* had given me a strong appreciation of this talented man and I enjoyed finding out more about his life. The tour was fun, giving performances at public concert halls, colleges and schools around the Brisbane area. Best of all, I was able to renew my friendship with Ron Forbes and enjoyed playing the odd trick or two for old times' sake. He still talks about one particularly foolish prank. A gardener was watering the grass outside the hotel with a long hose; I waited till he was moving the hose and switched it on unexpectedly. The man turned round in a rage to see Ron innocently standing next to the tap, unaware of the stunt that had been pulled on him. Exit Ron pursued by irate gardener.

Music festivals began to feature in my schedule that summer. There are a surprising number in the British Isles, and I enjoy the opportunity to perform in front of an audience, try out new pieces and techniques, and see what's going on in the music world. I gave a recital in a marquee at the Henley Festival on 11 July (great on atmosphere, not so good on acoustics!), followed by a more formal performance at the Chichester Festival three days later, in the Church of St Paul and St Peter the Great.

I was accompanied at Chichester by Robert Howie, a music lecturer from Aberdeen College of Education who frequently partnered me when Philip wasn't available, and we played pieces that were by now becoming part of my standard repertoire. These included one of the Sonatas for Timpani written by John Beck, an American percussionist and timpanist, and also a respected teacher. He is currently president of the Percussive Arts Society and a dear friend. Alfred Fissinger's Suite for Marimba is well known as one of the most difficult pieces for this instrument, requiring expert four-mallet work and control. I also played Fritz Kreisler's *Tambourin Chinois*, a work composed for the violin which adapts very nicely to the marimba or xylophone. I introduced all the works myself, establishing a rapport with the audience by little jokes: 'This is the part I find most difficult!' as I tuned the timpani, and encouraging them to enjoy the fireworks in Beck, 'It may not be everyone's cup of tea, but it isn't very often you see a solo timpanist – and a female one at that!'

Selecting what to play for an audience is almost as important as how well one performs. I take care to choose pieces that I think the audience will enjoy, but once the decision has been made I don't worry in advance about what the audience will think of me. Actually I love having an audience, I need that buzz in order to perform well. If the audience is slow to react, it's such uphill work and even if they then give me a standing ovation at the end, it doesn't mean as much as having the audience with me through the performance. There are ways, of course, of helping an audience to feel in a responsive mood right from the start. I try to walk on stage with a 'Hello, how are you?' approach, to make them feel enthusiastic and warm. Percussion is a very energetic medium and the fact that I am quite small but bounce around the instruments, using my body a lot and producing all this sound, can make an audience feel freer to respond actively, although British audiences are always subdued compared with what I have experienced in Brazil – or even North America. My efforts at both the festivals proved worthwhile. 'Performance was a gem' and 'Marimba magic' enthused the reviewers.

In August *Good Vibrations*, Yorkshire Television's short documentary about me in the *First Tuesday* series, was screened, in conjunction with another short film about a remarkable 70-year-old woman who lives alone in a bamboo shack in a jungle clearing deep in the heart of Belize. I thought Nick Gray had made a good job of directing and producing the documentary, which involved such excitements in our quiet neighbourhood as the cameraman balancing on a giant crane so he could film me playing the drums in my bedroom at Savernake Road, but I was amazed by the enormous amount of press attention that it received.

My own thoughts were now firmly set on Japan. I had recently received another grant, a surprise travel award of £500 from Opportunities for the Disabled, which was presented at the House of Commons at a reception hosted by Edward Heath. After a brief visit to Edinburgh to play in the festival with the trumpeter John Wallace and his ensemble The Wallace Collection, I was off again, en route for Hong Kong. This time I was travelling entirely alone and had to make my way first to Tokyo, and then to New York for a few days of recitals with James Blades. By now, however, I was an old hand at travel. The experiences of the past few months had given me confidence in my ability to cope even with the unexpected, and I was full of excitement at the prospect of seeing Keiko again and enjoying the novelty of Tokyo. I was to need all my optimism and fortitude, not to mention some of that good old Glennie determination. My stay in Japan was to stretch my resources – and my purse – to the limit, and a rather more worldly Evelyn would return to London, to reflect on the multifariousness of folk and experiences. 'Life's rich tapestry' – I certainly was about to experience it to the full.

19

The Glennie determination

'It is easier to understand a nation by listening to its music than by learning its language.'

Anon

Going to Japan to work with Keiko was the realization of one of my greatest ambitions. I so much wanted to improve my marimba work, as well as find out more about the Japanese way of feeling music, which I sensed was somehow different from the way it is experienced in the west. I had discovered a little more about Keiko's background, and knew that she had studied percussion with some of the great Japanese exponents, and composition with Minoru Miki and Akira Miyoshi whose works I was keen to explore further. She played the marimba for the Tokyo Quintet, and had a reputation as a teacher and composer of merit. My own brief experiences of her had confirmed that she had much to offer, and I could hardly wait to arrive in Tokyo, roll up my sleeves and get down to work.

The flight to Hong Kong was very pleasant, stopping at Bombay where I stretched my legs and bought a set of Indian bongos in one of the duty-free shops. I noticed that the airport seemed rather primitive, with splashes of green countryside to be seen between the shacks and derelict buildings. Hong Kong was very different, with a modern airport, where I was met by helpful tour operators and taken to the Holiday Inn Harbour View

Hotel. The facilities here were sumptuous and included a well-stocked mini-bar. I stuck to mineral water, much needed in the humidity, which even air-conditioning can't quite dispel. A walk round the shops in the evening to buy a few gifts and then I fell into bed exhausted, to watch *Dynasty* on my multi-channel television. I felt like a queen.

My arrival in Tokyo was less auspicious. For an hour before we landed the plane tossed and shook so much that even the stewardesses were frightened, and an American sitting near me declared that we were finished! I have never been so relieved to see trees and houses on either side of the plane and was grateful to set foot on the firm ground. My sensitivity to vibration is so acute that I quickly identify any change in engine activity, and am clutching my seat long before anyone else is aware that something is wrong. On this occasion I had several hundred terrified passengers to keep me company. I was met at the airport by my hostess, Mrs Ito, but it wasn't until we were in her car that I realized that she didn't speak a word of English. My months of struggling with the unfamiliar sounds and grammar of Japanese were going to come in useful sooner than I had anticipated. I had plenty of time to think up a few things to try out on Mrs Ito; the traffic was so bad that the drive into town seemed to last forever!

I had arranged with Keiko that three weeks would be a good time to spend in Tokyo. Apparently it was difficult to find accommodation, but she had managed to find the Ito family who were prepared to put me up – for what seemed to me a rather substantial fee. In fact everything was so expensive in Tokyo that I soon gave up even noticing the relative cost of living, and had to contact Kaye Artists to arrange for more funds alarmingly early in my trip.

With the Ito family I met my Waterloo. There were three generations living together, grandparents, Mr and Mrs Ito, and their son and daughter. The children could manage a few words of English, but their pronunciation was so odd that it was difficult for me to lip-read. The rest of the family spoke not a word. Worse than that, most of the family lacked those other essential components for communication – an interest in their fellow beings, and any basic good will. The only person who responded to me with warmth and generosity was the old grandfather; he had a twinkle in his eye that immediately made me feel at home, and I had some fun with him and his ever-poised camera.

The old folks were quite different from the younger generation; they wore traditional Japanese dress and ate sitting crosslegged on the floor. The house was large, with a lot of small rooms, so everyone had their own living places, and the grandparents didn't have the gadgets, the radio and television in every room, favoured by the younger Itos. It was extraordinary to see the layers in that family. The teenage children were so like the kids I knew at home, dressing in modern clothes and rushing off in their parents' car, and the son was a bit of a layabout, hanging around at home with his mates instead of going to college. Mrs Ito stayed at home to look after the house, but she obviously found it all a bit of a chore and spent most of her time watching television, while her husband appeared to devote every waking moment to his work.

With all that apparent leisure, one might have expected that Mrs Ito would have been available to help me find my way around the complexities of the Tokyo street system, never mind the tubes and buses, but no, this was not her intention. Apart from picking me up at the airport and (reluctantly) seeing me off again at the end of my stay, she never lifted a finger to help. This was particularly a problem when I set off to find Keiko's house for my first lesson. She lived on the opposite side of town and to get there I had to walk a while, take a train, take a bus, take a second bus and then try to hunt for Keiko's house in a district where there were no street names and the houses looked very similar. Needless to say, while my phrasebook Japanese might allow me to ask for directions, I couldn't understand the answers, and I spent a considerable amount of time wandering around in circles, unable to find my bearings.

I enjoyed some of the Ito household rituals, taking my shoes off before I went indoors, and eating whatever was put before me with interest if not always relish. The cold green tea was less to my liking, although I was intrigued by the Japanese tea ritual, which meant a substantial wait while the tea was prepared and served. There was no proper bathroom, just a rather primitive shower arrangement, but washing soon became an obsession as I woke up morning after morning with red itchy lumps all over my skin. Nobody knew quite what had caused these, although some insect was obviously having a good feast every night. Keiko bought me some ointment to stop the itching, and every night and morning the grandmother would ritually spray me with insect repellent, but nothing seemed to help. All you notice in Grandpa Ito's photos are my spotty legs!

My work with Keiko went very well indeed. She is the kind of musician I most admire, open and sensitive, and her priority is to communicate the feeling in a piece of music. What I worked on with her were not the techniques of playing the marimba as I had expected, but on understanding why and how pieces had been written. As a performer, Keiko works with a full range of styles of music, working out her own arrangements and adaptations of pieces. She has helped to develop Japanese music for the marimba by stimulating modern composers to produce works, many of which involve other instruments, so there are concertos for marimba, for strings and marimba, for four percussionists and marimba, saxophone or piano or oboe and marimba, and even full orchestral pieces with the marimba as solo instrument. For many of the solo marimba pieces, she had worked with the composer and knew about their ideas, and this knowledge made me interpret the pieces in new ways.

Modern Japanese music is very much influenced by western approaches, but there is something different and unique about it. I find it very easy to listen to and to learn, and once I have mastered a piece I never forget it. The music has everything in it; it's very emotional and atmospheric, and also very energetic, and even the quiet parts are full of tension. One of the differences between Japanese and western performers is the attitude to playing music. Japanese musicians don't regard performing as in any way a job or task that has to be got through; it is more a state of being, a total involvement, almost a religion. Music was an essential part of Keiko's life.

She also taught me how to use improvisation. I had begun to experiment with this when I was in Switzerland, but Keiko pushed me further. Her music room was tiny and we would stand facing one another, squeezed up against our five-octave Yamaha marimbas, and study a phrase of music for a while before closing the book and just playing around with the piece together. This free play made me pour out ideas and emotions that I hadn't realized were inside me, and taught me to appreciate the full range of the instrument. Keiko's most well-known piece, *Michi*, which is a standard favourite in my repertoire, was the result of an improvisation that she then wrote down. The word *michi* means 'path' or 'street', in Japanese, and she wrote the piece after a 'friend let her down', a 'social disappointment' as she describes it. The piece allows the performer to improvise for herself in certain sections, and invites the listener to explore the subtle melodies that are available beneath the surface of the marimba's more characteristically bold notes. When I play *Michi*, I use the idea of the path of the title, a path that goes right round the world, so that I begin with the typical intervals and sounds of Japanese music, but then bring in other harmonies, from the West, India, Latin America, until I finally return again to the idiom of Japan.

Keiko wasn't just a good teacher; she was also kind and generous, supportive about my financial anxieties – 'You can pay me later, when your money arrives' – and hospitable, inviting me to share meals with her husband and daughter. The Ito daughter had a marimba, so I was able to practise at my lodgings, and when I wasn't playing or travelling, I explored the shops, hunting for gifts for my family and looking at percussion instruments and music.

The Nippon Symphony Orchestra had a regular programme on Nippon Television, and I was invited to perform a ten-minute solo. The producer, a Mr Yui, came to the house to discuss the details with me and to tape a few samples of my playing. He didn't want anything heavyweight so we experimented with suitable pieces. Before he left he presented me with a Nippon Television watch, a rather masculine affair, and gave Mrs Ito a Nippon Television bath towel! 'Oh well,' I wrote in my diary, 'that certainly put some excitement in our day.'

On the day of the recording a very flash car arrived to take Mrs Ito, Grandpa and myself to the Nippon studio. A brass group were also playing and their timpanist presented me with his tartan stick holder. It was a bit like coals to Newcastle, but I was touched by his kind gesture. The main pieces filmed were *Czardas*, Chopin's Black Key Study and A Little Prayer, and solos for snare drum and timpani. Nippon Television had provided me with a good accompanist and I felt pleased with the results. Finally Mr Yui interviewed me, before presenting me with my fee, and sending us all home again in another grand car, although we stopped for some takeaway Kentucky Fried Chicken en route, which rather spoilt the effect. Later Grandpa and I went back to the studio to watch the film and I made plans with Mr Yui for a return visit. Grandpa had his photos of me at the studio developed and presented them to me in a little photo album. I was touched and delighted by his gift, a reminder of a happy day.

Another treat was a visit to the Yamaha factory producing tuned percussion, which Ronnie Cass had kindly arranged for me through a contact in the UK. The factory is some way outside Tokyo and gave me an opportunity to take the 'bullet' train through lush green mountains. I was able to see the instruments in various stages of manufacture and tried some of them out, mainly marimbas, vibraphones and timpani, as well as having a look round the piano factory. Despite hoping that I might be presented with a full concert grand marimba, I had to make do with two individual marimba bars, but came away well-satisfied with my day.

The Royal Opera House orchestra and singers were also in Tokyo at this time, so I was able to meet up with their percussionists, and see a marvellous performance of *Turandot*. I also met the Dutch percussionist Jan Pustjens, who was full of useful information about music and mallets, promising to send me catalogues, and inviting me to see a timpani factory in Holland. Needless to say, my attempts to establish contact with these people led to more frustration with the Itos. I had discovered that Mr Ito could in fact speak quite reasonable English, although he rarely used it, but when I asked him to explain how to get to Jan's hotel, he pretended not to understand and went on watching television. Mrs Ito's solution was that I should set off for my destination and ring the hotel if I had any problems! Maybe she hadn't noticed that I was deaf. 'If only I had a human family,' I wrote in my diary in pure rage that evening, then added 'maybe that's the problem — they *are* human.' Luckily I met enough friendly and helpful Japanese to realize I had just had bad luck with the Itos.

Despite these minor difficulties I enjoyed my stay in Tokyo. I benefited from my work with Keiko, but perhaps the greatest gain was the experience of travelling there alone and having to manage without anyone else to depend on. This was a huge leap forward in my self-confidence and independence. The rest of the trip promised only pleasure and I set off for New York on 24 September with excitement and optimism. I was about to re-encounter the friendly Americans and best of all to meet James Blades once more.

To my delight I arrived first and was able to meet him off his plane at New York's Kennedy airport, from where we flew together to Rochester. We visited the Eastman School of Music, where James gave a talk and we were able to rehearse for the two concerts that we had scheduled, one at Eastman and the other at the National Technical Institute for the Deaf, part of Rochester Institute for Technology. I met my old friends John Beck, who was teaching at Eastman and had arranged our visit, and Robert Zildjian of Sabian Cymbals, as well as many new contacts. The concerts were well-received, and it was a delight to be in this warm, friendly and musical atmosphere, which both James and I revelled in. We returned to New York together, where I saw James off on the plane to London. He insisted that I didn't wait until his flight was called, and I left him sitting on his suitcase, a tiny and forlorn figure, who had gallantly kissed my hand as we said goodbye. Dear James, my heart went out to him; he had all the energy and enthusiasm of a young man of 20, and I knew how much he enjoyed the excitement of being with our American friends, and how much he regretted having to leave it all behind.

I stayed on in New York for several days to give a recital arranged by Kaye Artists at St Paul's Chapel in Trinity Church on Wall Street. It was a lunch time concert and the audience were mainly people who had dropped in from work, but the percussionist Gordon

Gottlieb also attended. I regard him as a world class player and was delighted to meet him. Gordon is a great talker and enthusiast about percussion, and we spent as much time as possible together exchanging ideas before I left for London. He took me to see session work which he was involved with, and the New York Philharmonic and introduced me to their percussionists, who made me feel very welcome.

Finally it was time to go home. I packed my cases for the last time and boarded yet another jumbo. I had been away for just over a month, but it felt as if barely a week had passed as I settled in again to my room at Savernake Road and gave myself a big pat on the back for being so brave. One day I would travel the world again, but it would never seem quite such a challenge.

There was little time for self-congratulation. I had an engagement booked with John Wallace at the Nettlefold Festival in only six days time, and was soon busy rehearsing with him. John is an extraordinary trumpeter. He is principal trumpet with the Philharmonia and a member of Equale Brass and his own ensemble The Wallace Collection. He plays anything from baroque to contemporary, and the programme we put together included works by Tanaka, Jolivet and Paul Max Edlin. Jolivet's *Heptade* is a trumpet and percussion piece, difficult but rewarding, and great to play. *The Nocturnal Landscapes* were written specially for us by Paul Edlin, and I also had the opportunity to try out Souster's *Curtain of Light*, which involves percussion and taped music. This was quite a challenge for me as I couldn't hear when the tape sections started, so the tape operator had to guide me and I had to be meticulous about my timing.

John and I had another opportunity to play together later that month in Madrid with The Wallace Collection. There was little time to see the town as we spent our only full day there rehearsing for the concert which was one of a series and started at 10.30 in the evening.

We were all exhausted, but I decided to make a night of it with some of the percussionists who had attended our concert; I staggered back to the hotel at half past five in the morning ready for my 7 am flight.

The rest of the year was busy with engagements that varied from solos with the RTE Concert Orchestra in the National Concert Hall in Dublin when I played a variety of works, to a guest appearance on the *Val Doonican Christmas Show*. But change was in the air. Ann Rachlin had told me that her daughter wanted to sell the flat at Savernake Road, so I had three months notice to find somewhere new. I was also beginning to experience some differences of opinion with Kaye Artists about my future. Nina and her team had been terrific, but perhaps it was time for a change or even to manage myself for a while. I had also quite unexpectedly fallen in love with a young man whom I hoped to marry, and after some indecision I decided that after Christmas I would move to Surrey to live with him and his parents until we could find a home of our own.

None of this filled me with any foreboding and I ended the year as optimistically as I had begun it, but if I had had a crystal ball I might have seen challenges ahead that would test my courage and self-belief in far more painful ways than my experiences in Tokyo. My life was to know shadows as well as the bright sunlight that seemed to have blessed my activities up to this point and I was to emerge a sadder, wiser and stronger person.

20

A little sun, a little rain

> 'A musician cannot move others unless he himself is moved.'
>
> C P E Bach

The period that followed my move from Savernake Road was one of growth and change. So many good things happened, but there were also some bad moments. Like Keiko, I suffered a 'social disappointment.' My love affair came to nothing, and we parted with tears and regret and not inconsiderable pain. These things happen, but six months of hope were followed by a blanket of unhappiness of a kind I have never before experienced. Fortunately it passed and I came through, stronger and more self-aware, and more than ever determined to make music as fully, richly and honestly as I could.

There were also some changes on the professional front. I parted from Nina early in the year, reluctantly and with warm gratitude for all her wonderful support and the contacts and work she had brought my way, but we both felt it was time for a new direction. It was obviously impossible to run my professional life without expert help, and I was grateful when Jasper Parrott agreed to see me in the spring to talk about the possibility of representing me. I was attracted to Harrison/Parrott Management because they had excellent overseas contacts and took an international view in securing bookings for their musicians. This was important for me as Britain is only a small part of the great world of music, and I was sure that working abroad would help me to establish myself as a serious musician, and put me in touch with new ideas for percussion instruments and repertoire. I also liked the fact that they worked intensively with their clients. I wanted to branch out to include a wider range of concert and recital work, and also had ideas for television and the possibility of a recording contract. I needed help and guidance if I was to develop in all these different areas.

Jasper was initially cautious about the idea of representing me. Although I only discovered this later, he agreed to see me because he believes it is important to encourage young and promising artists, but he had no idea that he would actually take me on. The real problem for him was how to develop a satisfying career for a solo percussionist. Although I had by now had considerable success playing at many music clubs, and societies and festivals up and down the country, the sheer cost of transporting all the equipment I needed to and fro meant that this kind of engagement put a financial strain on the smaller groups who were keen to hire me. I needed to broaden my horizons and also to become the kind of household name that meant everyone would benefit from my performances. There was also the question of how to balance my 'popular' side with my career as a serious musician. Obviously my television work in particular indicated that all kinds of audiences took an interest in me and that my future did not lie solely on the formal concert platform. All this had to be thought through before Jasper could agree to take me on.

Fortunately our first meeting went extremely well and Jasper claims he was bowled over by my dynamic personality! I certainly felt able to share my ideas and ambitions with him, and to my great joy, after several weeks of looking into the possibilities, he eventually said yes, he would represent me. We have worked together ever since, and he and his team have been personally as well as professionally supportive.

When I left Surrey in the middle of the year, I was able to rent Jasper's flat in West London while I was waiting to buy my own home; it was very near to his house and comforting to know that he was around the corner while I was adjusting to living on my own for the first time. In fact, I loved being by myself. No need to worry about practising at odd hours or having to be sociable when I wanted to work. Now I have my own flat with a cellar studio for my instruments which is more or less soundproof. I have had one complaint, however; one day a scribbled note came through the letterbox: 'I am your nabour (sic) and your confounded noise of so-called music is driving me mad. . . .' Oh dear, obviously not a paid-up member of the Evelyn Glennie fan club.

Work is a great panacea and I was helped through these sometimes difficult times by a series of interesting and challenging engagements. In January, I gave my first performance of Stockhausen's *Zyklus* as part of a London Sinfonietta concert series, Response, at the Queen Elizabeth Hall. This is a popular work with percussionists, and perhaps for that reason I tend to avoid it, but it was good to have the opportunity to try it out. The critics were kind. Dominic Gill in *The Financial Times* said that my performance was 'an electrifying *tour de force* – delivered with marvellous energy and concentration, and with powerful dramatic presence.' Robert Henderson in *The Daily Telegraph* called it a 'stunning performance', and Paul Griffiths of *The Times* wrote that it was 'clear, confident and compelling'.

In March there was the official first performance of *Rags to Riches*, a work commissioned specially for me from the composer Malcolm Singer with funds provided by the Greater London Arts. I had become interested in Malcolm's work when I saw a video of his *Man versus Machine*, a music-theatre piece which involves a master of ceremonies, percussionist and computer-generated tape. We spent some time working out ways in which I could work with the tape, experimenting with an ingenious electrical device, worn on the wrist, which would indicate what was happening on the tape so that I knew when to come in with my parts. With *Rags to Riches*, we agreed that I should be given the opportunity to play many different instruments and to demonstrate my virtuosity and musicianship. The work progresses through tom-toms, temple blocks, cowbells and cymbals to xylophone, marimba, vibraphone and glockenspiel and mark tree.

I continued to play with The Wallace Collection and had a memorable concert with them, again at The Queen Elizabeth Hall, performing the Czech composer Dalibor Vačkář's Concerto for Trumpet, Keyboards and Percussion. The pianist was the late John Ogdon. I was intrigued by his personality as he seemed to live in a world of his own until he played, when I felt we communicated on familiar territory. Vačkář was a great anglophile, the proud owner of a Dunhill pipe which probably inspired his Smoking Symphony, and a fan of George Bernard Shaw. The Concerto for Trumpet was completed in 1963 and features a range of percussion instruments and some lively stickwork, and I later recorded it for Nimbus Records at Henry Wood Hall.

John and I played together again a few weeks later at the Arnolfini Theatre in Bristol, a chance to polish my performance of *Zyklus*. Indeed, one of the most gratifying aspects of my work at this time was that I was being invited to return to venues where I had previously given successful performances, and to play concertos again with orchestras and ensembles who had worked with me in the past. I returned to my own territory in May for a Prom concert at the Aberdeen Music Hall with the Scottish National Orchestra. Milhaud's Concerto for Marimba, Vibraphone and Orchestra is an exotic work, influenced by the composer's experience of the rhythms and colours of Latin-American music when he was working in Brazil in the late 1890s. The piece makes use of Latin themes, and whilst not strongly melodic, offers an opportunity for technical skill and depth of feeling. The other work I played was my own arrangement for marimba and orchestra of Saint-Saëns' Introduction and *Rondo Capriccioso*, a stylish composition requiring some agility from the soloist.

With thoughts of a return to North America for Pasic '87, I was pleasantly surprised to win the Leonardo da Vinci prize for the most outstanding musician of 1987, which was awarded by eight European Rotary Clubs. Sir Yehudi Menuhin presented me with the certificate and a cheque for £3,000 at a special ceremony at the Barbican Centre, and I made a little speech and played *Michi* on the marimba. I also attended the Wavendon Allmusic Awards which are administered by a trust founded by Cleo Laine and Johnny Dankworth, and are intended to recognize musical achievement across a broad range of amateur and professional music activities. I was to work with John Dankworth later that year at the Barbican Summer Pops, with the London Symphony Orchestra and the brilliant jazz pianist George Shearing.

Another musical first was the premiere of the Scottish composer John McLeod's Percussion Concerto on a tour with the National Youth Orchestra of Scotland. This piece was specially written for me by John, whom I had first met as a schoolgirl when I performed in his work *The Gokstad Ship* in 1982. We had great fun working on the concerto. As with any new percussion composition, a prime consideration was how many percussion instruments would be required and how they would be organized on the stage, particularly how to allow for the fact that the work might be played on smaller stages as well as in large concert halls. I suggested to John that he write for marimba, snare drum and possibly timpani. 'Fine, let's keep it to a minimum.' However, as the concept developed, John introduced more and more instruments, and by the end we had an array that took a fair while to set up, not to mention occupying a large proportion of even a capacious stage. John's programme note describes the work as 'inspired by the artistry of Evelyn Glennie'. The idea is that I gradually emerge from the orchestra to perform as a soloist. I start by playing in a team of three timpanists, but gradually move out on my own to play increasingly virtuoso music on a vast array of instruments.

It is a demanding piece requiring the stamina of a top athlete – but we percussionists need that anyway. Even though I had moved to West London by this time, early morning jogs and lots of vegetables were still an essential part of my routine. I reckoned they compensated for the late nights I so much enjoyed, 'newsing' with other musicians after an evening's performance.

These were wonderful opportunities to explore new works, new interpretations, and to develop my flexibility in adapting to different orchestras, ensembles, conductors and venues. But I hadn't forgotten old favourites, and I was delighted when the opportunity came for a new performance of Bartók's Sonata for Two Pianos and Percussion. Indeed, who wouldn't have been? I was to perform on tour with Sir Georg Solti and Murray Perahia, and we were to record the work for CBS records. David Corkhill, a teacher at the Guildhall School of Music and Drama, was the timpanist and Craig Sheppard, the American pianist, played at two of the performances in place of Murray Perahia. The tour was spread over several days, beginning in Oxford at the Sheldonian Theatre, and included performances in Schwetzingen in Germany, Zürich, Paris and London, and at the Aldeburgh Festival. Sir Georg knew the work well; he had turned the pages for Bartók when the composer had performed the piece many years previously. I found him so modest; the sonata is very difficult for pianists, and at rehearsals Sir Georg would exclaim, 'Oh, my wooden fingers won't go any faster!' when he came to a particularly tricky section, which made us all laugh and relax. It was interesting to see the difference in the way he worked with his two fellow pianists. The piece is so rich and demanding, and even the change of one person in the quartet can have a substantial effect on how it is interpreted and played.

I bought a special evening gown for the tour, a long dress in black velvet with a gold pattern, a gold band round the tightly fitting waist and a full skirt so I could move freely. All the men were in dress suits, so I wanted to blend in and yet look very feminine. The reviews were terrific and I even stole a little of the limelight from Sir Georg, to Jasper's delight: 'Evelyn Glennie . . . twirling and flourishing in a breathtaking xylophone solo, even managed to steal the show for a moment from the Hungarian maestro,' wrote the critic from *Tages-Anzeiger*.

The record was released early in 1988 along with a television documentary about the making of it to mark the fiftieth anniversary of the work, and in 1989 it was awarded a Grammy Award by the National Academy of Recording Arts and Sciences in California. This was a great honour, which was enormously appreciated by my American friends. Gordon Gottlieb wrote an ecstatic note: 'I assume that you know what the Grammy Awards are here . . . the MAJOR music achievement honors. All of your names were flashed across the TV screens in *thousands* of American homes.' Robert Zildjian sent a list of the winners, so I could see how 'our little Scot sweetheart . . . scored in the Grammy polls'. He added, 'Sir Georg deserves a pat also, but we'll leave that up to you!' I had in fact met up again with Sir Georg in the October after the recording, when I appeared on the edition of *This is Your Life* devoted to him. Sir Georg made a joke about my turning up on time. Rather embarrassingly I had arrived a few minutes

THE
**NATIONAL ACADEMY OF RECORDING
ARTS & SCIENCES, INC.**
CORDIALLY INVITES YOU TO ATTEND
**THE 31ST
ANNUAL GRAMMY® AWARDS**
WEDNESDAY, FEBRUARY 22, 1989
IN LOS ANGELES

late for two of the rehearsals for the Bartók owing to the problem of driving into London from Surrey during the rush hour. I hate being unpunctual, but it is luckily a rare occurrence, and Sir Georg's friendly hug suggested that he had forgiven me.

Pasic '87 was in St Louis and I had a wonderful trip, again reducing the audience to tears and laughter. I love the way American audiences respond with so much emotion; the only problem is that I find myself sobbing in sympathy! My friend Lauren Vogel took the opportunity to interview me for *Modern Drummer* magazine and wrote a lengthy article which was published in the May 1989 edition. It is a sensitive piece, dealing with many aspects of performance and technique, and John Beck, the president of Percussive Arts Society, wrote to the magazine to express his appreciation. At the end of the convention I walked along the Mississippi river, enjoying the warm air and tranquil water, while the streets alongside were thronged with people celebrating Hallowe'en. I felt warmed and invigorated by being with my American friends again, my mind whizzing with new ideas and my fingers itching to try them out. It's impossible to feel anything but exhilarated at Pasic, and the feeling kept me going through the beginning of the English winter.

Fortunately there were other treats to follow. I was invited to perform in the Young Musicians slot at the Royal Variety Performance at the London Palladium. Afterwards I was introduced to the Queen, who asked me whether I needed to be strong to play. She had obviously been impressed by my athletic rendering of *Tambourin Chinois*! It was a terrific experience, but I was disappointed that the Young Musician slot had to be cut out of the television transmission as the show had run significantly over time. I had another encounter with royalty at the end of the year, at a Beethoven Fund concert at the Barbican. This time I was in the audience, watching Prince Edward narrate the text of Prokofiev's *Peter and the Wolf*, played by the LSO with Ezra Rachlin conducting. There were lots of children at the concert and I had fun at the reception playing Jingle Bells with a group of excited deaf youngsters.

'One more year of awareness and experience', I wrote in my diary on 31 December; but my spirits were high and I felt ready for anything. I was soon to move into my new flat and my schedule for 1988 already looked crowded. Somehow I had survived the turmoil and had had a year of quite outstanding music; what I had to do now was to build on this solid foundation, and I felt confident that I would do just that. In less than three years I had established myself as a solo performer; the question was, what should I aim for next?

21

Musical milestones

'In the performance you have to *be* the composer: "This is *my* music, part of my body – it belongs to *me*." '

Carlo Maria Giulini

Having proved that I could make a living for myself as a solo percussionist, it was time both to enjoy my developing reputation and to look for new challenges. I love live performances and was eager to expand my programme of engagements as a musician, and to enlarge the repertoire of music that I could offer to concert organizers. I had also long had the ambition to establish myself as a recording artist, and was interested in building on my work with television. All these areas offered different opportunities, but I was so full of energy that I felt I could cope with the versatility required to adapt to the varying styles of presentation and performance. None of these aims could be fulfilled immediately, of course; each required planning and work, but as the months passed my efforts in all three directions began to bear fruit.

Every day was busy, studying new music and practising for performances, travelling to and from my increasing number of engagements in the UK and beginning, excitingly, to be invited to perform overseas. I also had to attend to my voluminous correspondence (I still reply personally to all fan mail), and find the time to shop for concert clothes and have my hair done. Amidst all this rush of activity, I also tried to make sure that I had the odd moment to be absolutely quiet and peaceful, to remind myself of who I was and what I was trying to achieve. I believe this kind of spiritual replenishment is as important to my ability to function as a musician as studying music and practising.

Clothes were important. With the help of Nina and the television wardrobe ladies who had accompanied me on shopping trips, I had begun to take an informed interest in my personal appearance, but by now I was confident enough to develop a style that I felt combined good looks with comfort. When I first began giving concerts and recitals, I usually wore a long dress or skirt, because that was the convention, but I began to feel increasingly uncomfortable in clothes and shoes that restricted my freedom of movement. I like to express my personality through my clothes as well as my speech and music, and I like people to feel that they can approach me afterwards to talk about the performance; too formal a presentation might inhibit them from doing this. I started to choose shorter dresses for less formal occasions, and for recital work I moved into trousers, often cut along Japanese lines so that they flowed without hindering my movements in any way. For concertos, where I am performing with an orchestra in a formal context, I abide by the conventions and wear glamorous gowns, but they have to be properly cut so that I can move without worrying that a strapless top is going to pop off, or a too-tight skirt will split when I make a particularly energetic movement! And I do kick off my high heels whenever I can. . . .

I enjoy all my professional engagements and try to give of my best, however humble the occasion; however there were some musical milestones during this very busy period. I had first worked with the Scottish Chamber Orchestra the previous August and was delighted when they invited me back for a Royal Gala at the Guildhall in London, attended by their patron the Prin-

cess of Wales. John Wallace was playing the Mozart
Trumpet Concerto, and I had the privilege of being
conducted by George Malcolm. It was a glittering
occasion in the beautiful surroundings of the Guildhall.
After the performance, I was re-introduced to Princess
Diana – having met her once before – and we had a
relaxed and delightful talk. Later I sat at dinner with
one of her bodyguards, who told me some interesting
stories about his work.

Another sparkling evening was a performance with
the English Chamber Orchestra conducted by the
extremely charming Jeffrey Tate at the Festival Hall.
This was the annual Sir John Barbirolli Concert, sponsored by the Royal Philharmonic Society, who aim to
present one major young artist at each event, so it
was a great honour to be invited to perform. I played
Milhaud's Concerto for Marimba, Vibraphone and
Orchestra, which had a mixed reception from the critics, but they were kind about my performance. Geoffrey
Norris in *The Daily Telegraph* wrote that the Milhaud
'gave a welcome chance to hear the brilliance of Miss
Glennie's talent.' Edward Greenfield in *The Guardian*
again felt I made the best of the music, using the marimba to bring out its poetry, and adding, 'it was a
delight to watch Miss Glennie leaping from one keyboard to another, changing sticks, or even reversing
them and for a moment or two using the handles
instead.' A more personal accolade came from David
Robinson, who attended the concert with his wife and
wrote me a treasured note to say how much they had
enjoyed the occasion, and how proud and pleased they
were for me.

I received another letter from David soon afterwards,
congratulating me on having been elected an Associate
of the Royal Academy of Music. This is offered to
students who the Academy feels have distinguished
themselves in the profession, and it is very rare for a
young musician to receive the honour – I was still only

22. On the letter from the directors I scribbled a little note to myself: 'I'm travelling towards my aims in life, and towards perfection as a musician.' I felt as strongly as ever the wish to improve the quality of my work and to develop my musicianship, and each step along the way was both a joy and an incentive to try even harder to achieve the standards I had set myself.

I often refer to the lighter pieces of music in my repertoire as 'lollipops', enjoyable trifles which don't make too many demands. Whilst I don't regard any recital as an opportunity to relax, I do like to have lighter moments among my engagements, times when I can be myself and communicate with the audience in a lighthearted way, perhaps experimenting with new repertoire or trying out new combinations of music on the programme. Meeting new people is such a vital part of my enjoyment of performing, and I love the opportunity for informal encounters.

One such opportunity came in May when I was invited with Philip to give a recital at All Saints Leamington Hastings, the first in the concert series held every year at this charming church in Warwickshire. I had a lovely time introducing the repertoire and making the audience laugh, and during the interval we ate strawberries and cream, the trademark of the series, in the garden of a neighbouring house, strolling about and enjoying the marvellous warm weather. The organizer, Ray Law, introduced me to so many people that I hardly had time to eat my strawberries; I can't eat and watch people's faces at the same time, which has meant many a frustrating cold meal with chatterboxes! Ray was inundated with letters afterwards from people who had enjoyed the concert, and he was kind enough to send me copies. I was so happy to know that everyone had enjoyed the music and the informal way I presented it – a wonderful occasion which I've been delighted to be invited to repeat every year since.

Another very different and unusual opportunity arose

always been interested in giving
ad mentioned this to Catherine
tional Director of the Scottish
ho arranged for me to give a
en Prison. This is an all-male
norities had reservations. Poss-
ught I would be presenting a heavily classi-
ogramme that would not prove attractive to the
inmates, and they may also have wondered how a young
female performer would cope with a possibly hostile or
disruptive audience. However, in the end arrangements
were made, and I arrived to find a group of some sixty
men in a very large hall, with a number of prison staff
to keep an eye on everything. It was an afternoon recital
and attendance wasn't compulsory, the men could get
up and leave at any time, but I hoped to keep their
attention by a lively and mixed programme, with some
'lollipop' pieces as well as more serious and emotional
works.

At first I was a little daunted since many of the men
looked quite tough and sat slouched in the rather
uncomfortable-looking metal chairs, but I was determined to win them over, chatting in a relaxed and
informal way as I presented the array of instruments
and making little jokes to keep the atmosphere light
and fun. To my delight, at the end of half an hour they
were sitting forward in their seats attentively and no
one got up to leave. At the end of the ninety-minute
session I asked whether there were any more questions,
and one man stood up and said, 'We've nothing more
to ask – just play.' The way he said it was one the
greatest compliments I've ever received.

Afterwards I had a chance to meet the men, and one
of them helped me to dismantle my instruments. He
told me that the prison had only recently started having
people in for talks on a variety of subjects and that it
had had a significant effect on morale. The men looked
forward to the talks and felt they had a new interest in

life. By this time I had almost forgotten that [...] prison, but as we were chatting, the prison [...] stepped up rather briskly to join us; after my [...] had left I happened to ask why he was there. Appar[...] he had committed a number of crimes against wom[...] and several of the audience had quite disturbing histor[...] ies of violence. I was astonished by this, as they had been so responsive and interested in the recital.

After this I was determined to give more lecture recitals in prisons and in July 1989 arranged visits to Wormwood Scrubs and Holloway Prison through Gillian Moore from the London Sinfonietta. I went to Wormwood Scrubs with a van full of instruments driven by my roadie, Tony Davenport, but we had some trouble getting through the gate. The guard had not been warned about my visit and refused to let me in. He was a tall thickset man with a bullying manner, and obviously did not feel that he had to treat this young woman with any respect. That kind of attitude makes me very angry, so it was another occasion for standing as tall as my small stature will allow, squaring my shoulders and shouting back. The noise attracted another guard, who eventually let me in for the inevitable security check. To my surprise the recital was held in a beautiful chapel in the grounds of the prison, a bright modern building with wonderful acoustics. The performance went well and I went on talking and playing for two hours. Afterwards I had tea with the inmates, who were sympathetic about my problems gaining access and commented on the brutalizing effects of being 'inside', the lack of freedom and human respect. One man had written the words for a song and asked for help to put them to music; another was saying that there were some good aspects to life inside and he pointed out the paintings round the walls of the chapel, all done by inmates of their own faces. While we talked, guards stood by with dogs, which seemed so incongruous in a chapel, and at a fixed time the men were led away to be locked up for the night.

After my Prom I received a letter from a man in Leyhill Prison saying how much he had liked my performance and mentioning a group called The Offenders that he was involved with. A few days later I happened to see this group publicized on Breakfast TV. I wrote to the man to thank him and to say I knew about his group, who were rather good; it seemed strange to have to write a number as well as his name on the envelope.

Experiencing the good side of people in this way, whilst also knowing the reasons why some of them are in prison and reading in the papers the kind of horrific crime committed day after day, leaves me with a sense of doubt and confusion. I don't know what the proper care of criminals should be, but I do have a wish to visit as many English-speaking prisons as I can, both in the UK and overseas, to share the very positive experience of making music and talking to the inmates about their responses to it.

My visit to Holloway Women's Prison was rather different. The women I met did not appear to be violent or serious criminals, and the regime was more liberal with excellent library and sports facilities, no uniforms, no feeling that staff were watching their every move. It was rather like a school, except that every time you walked through a door someone had to unlock it and lock it again behind you. Many of the women were foreigners who had been caught trying to smuggle drugs through customs, often acting as couriers for serious drug traffickers. They were a far less peaceful audience than the male prisoners; somebody was always getting up and walking around, and women sitting together chatted and argued throughout the recital. I felt that the atmosphere was less competitive than in the male prisons, so that the women operated more as a group and felt free to express their responses rather than huddling on their own or in a tiny gang. Despite the rowdiness, a good time was had by all, and I enjoyed the challenge of trying to hold the attention of this rather unruly gathering.

Music festivals are also occasions to meet new people and try out new ideas. Many of them take place during the summer, and offer a marvellous excuse to explore new parts of Britain when the countryside is looking its best. I performed in the Fishguard, Bradford and Salisbury Festivals, winning the striking review headline from the latter, 'Glennie moves audience from tears to terror'! I felt rather flattered, but wondered which part of the programme had been quite so frightening.

I also had two recitals at the Edinburgh Festival with the Scottish free-bass accordionist Owen Murray in August. Owen is as determined to win acceptance for the free bass accordion as I am to establish percussion, and became the first Professor of the subject at the Royal Academy of Music in 1986. The concert was part of the twenty-first birthday celebrations of The Lamp of Lothian Collegiate Trust, which is chaired by the Duchess of Hamilton, and aims to restore buildings in Haddington and use them to promote the arts, and youth and community activities. I have played at Trust concerts several years running, often performing in St Mary's Parish Church, Haddington, a mediaeval church which the Trust has helped to restore. Lady Elizabeth and her son Lord Patrick are always very supportive and hospitable; I stayed with them for the performance in Haddington, and Patrick and their driver, Jimmy, drove me to Edinburgh airport, which was a great relief as I was exhausted after a series of late nights and strenuous practice with Owen of some unfamiliar repertoire.

I had won the Wavendon Young Professional Allmusic Musician of the Year Award for 1988 and in September was guest performer at the Trust's Royal Charity Gala Concert at the Barbican Hall. Princess Margaret was the royal guest; she was very pleasant and said that she had been worried I might have been stuck in the malfunctioning lift because I arrived a little late at the reception.

The final outstanding event of that year was a trip to Norway to play with the Trondheim Symfoniorkester. It was the first time that I had played with the orchestra and that they had featured a solo percussionist. The fact that we had a Russian conductor, Juozas Domarkas, added to the international flavour. The audience were overwhelmingly appreciative and I came home after three days of kindness and good music feeling so high that my feet barely touched the ground. The King of Norway was on the flight back to London, which seemed somehow appropriate to my elevated state of mind.

The year ended with an affectionate note from Ronnie Cass, my friend from *Highway*. 'Dear Evelyn,' he wrote, 'I would just like you to be aware, that after knowing you slightly longer than five years, I am more than ever convinced that you are the most remarkable person I have ever met in my life.' He added, more prosaically, 'This does not mean that I will not continue to treat you as rubbish. . . .'

In the meantime I had been working on how I might develop my work for television. Early in 1989, thanks to Jasper, I was offered a tremendous opportunity to pursue several of my enthusiasms simultaneously. I was invited to travel to Rio de Janeiro to explore the kinds of instruments used in Brazilian percussion and to join the *Carnaval*, a feast of colour, rhythm and sound that was to be one of the great experiences of my life and would have a profound effect on my music.

22

Carnaval

'A vida e um sonho,
E o sonho ilusão . . .'

In the words of the Brazilian *sambista*, life is a dream
and the dream itself a mirage. The few days I spent in
Rio de Janeiro in February 1989 participating in the
extraordinary *Carnaval* celebrations had all the colour,
incident and exoticism of a spectacular fantasy.

Carnival is principally celebrated in Europe. The
name probably comes from the Latin term *carne-vale*,
'farewell to meat', and the festivities take place before
Lent, an opportunity to eat, drink and generally have
fun before the austerity of fast. In Brazil the *Carnaval*
lasts for four days of frenetic activity, when even the
poorest slum-dwellers are able to forget the harsh realit-
ies of their lives and dress up as anyone or thing they
wish to be – emperor or queen, clown or fluffy animal,
resplendent in spangles and feathers, or their own
flamboyant nudity. I had read about *Carnaval* and had
often longed to go; a conversation between Jasper Parrott and Chris Hunt of Iambic Productions paved the
way.

The idea was that Chris should make a film about
me for London Weekend Television's *South Bank
Show*, the Sunday arts programme presented by Melvyn
Bragg. The documentary was to deal with my life and
background, but primarily it was to centre around the
Carnaval in Brazil, and to show me trying out some of

the instruments in the Brazilian percussion family and joining in the great Parade, playing *samba* music with one of the many *escolas de samba*, the samba schools who compete in the *Carnaval* league table.

Samba is now the major force behind *Carnaval*. Originating in the dance rhythms of the black Angolan slaves who were brought to Brazil in the sixteenth century by Portuguese settlers, it incorporated the Catholic rituals of the colonists, producing a rich blend of pagan and Christian practices that are still observed by the *samba* schools. There are more than twenty of these in Rio, each containing a number of *Carnaval* groups, who are graded into eight sections, rather like a football league, with the best groups in the top division being invited to perform in the Parade.

In a city where eight million poor are crowded into slums and *favelas*, the shanty towns, while a wealthy few live in elegant luxury in the Copacabana and Ipanema coastal resorts, the preparations for *Carnaval* represent total commitment, a year of scrimping and saving to buy costumes, and hours of practice with a *samba* school. The schools include *bateria* (percussion section), dance groups and singers, and many composers who write hundreds of *sambas*, which are rehearsed for several months before one is selected for the Parade. Each *samba* tells a story, and provides an opportunity for political jokes and satire. Once a *samba* has been chosen, the school can decide on the theme of its presentation and get busy designing costumes for the different groups, each of which will parade on foot or on elaborately decorated floats along the two-mile parade route. The Parade is competitive and groups have to operate within strict rules relating to costume, presentation, time-keeping and so on. Any infringement means a loss of points, so everyone is on their best behaviour, and the groups vie to move up the league or at least to maintain their position.

Because *Carnaval* has become so much the means by

which the poor of the town can express their individuality and identity, *samba* groups gather in bars and on the streets throughout the year to play the dominant *samba* beat and remind themselves that good times are just around the corner – even if they will end almost as soon as they begin. This street-corner rhythm was what I noticed most about my time in Brazil; give a *samba* player a box of matches and in seconds he'll turn out the catchiest beat.

It is very rare for a non-Brazilian to join the Parade; my American friend Gordon Gottlieb had managed it, but would Chris be able to secure me a much-covered place in a *samba* school? With the help of Gita Englehart, a Brazilian production manager whom Chris knew, an approach was made – and accepted, and soon after the plan had first been discussed I found myself on a plane to Rio, bound for a week of rhythm and anything but the blues.

Typical *samba* instruments include *tamborim, pandeiro, agogo* bells, the *ganza* or shaker family, and various drums such as the *cuica, caixa* and the *surdo*, a massive drum rather like a cross between a very large tom-tom and a bass drum. However, as I would have to carry my instrument for nearly two hours in the Parade, we decided that I should probably stick to a small light instrument such as the *agogo* bells, which are handheld, or the *tamborim*, a small single-headed drum, which is held in one hand and beaten with a small drumstick or several connected plastic rods, to make a terrific noise like the rattle of a machine gun. Soon after I arrived in Rio, Alan Hayman from the London School of Samba took me on a shopping expedition to select my instrument for the *bateria* and we decided that the *tamborim* was the best choice. All I had to do was to learn to play it!

Although there are basically only five sounds to learn on the instrument, they involve some manual dexterity both in isolation and even more when played in sequence and in the *samba* rhythm, and my major concern was that I wouldn't be able to master the more complex twiddles in time. If a judge caught me fluffing my strokes, all would be up for the *bateria*, so I was determined to get it right. Every spare moment was spent practising in the hotel, a plush establishment in the tourist centre of Rio, with magnificent balcony views of the sea and comfortable air-conditioned rooms.

My room was next door to Mike Fox the cameraman, whose attempts to catnap during the day were ruined by my vigorous *rat-a-tat-tat*. After a while I took pity on him and practised in the bathroom, but this didn't completely deaden the racket. One morning I was in full beat when I became aware of a disturbance at the door. The jetlagged traveller did not mince his words. 'Can you please shut up,' he yelled in English; 'I'm trying to get some sleep!' I didn't hesitate. 'Do you know who I am?' I enquired, drawing myself up to my full five foot two; '*I* am Brazil's top *tamborim* player.' Splendidly haughty, I slammed the door in his face and withdrew to the bathroom, where I meekly placed a towel over the *tamborim* to try to muffle the sound. There were no more interruptions.

My introduction to the *samba* school, the *Unidos do Cabuçu*, came just three days before the procession. Rehearsals were held in an open air school, where over 2000 dancers and a hundred percussionists got together to try out their chosen *samba*. The volume of noise issuing from all these people was so powerful that it felt almost like a rain of bullets pushing me back against the wall. The greatest noise came from the *surdo*, but the combined effect of all the players and singers was equally overwhelming. The *tamborim* players didn't know anything about me, and were rather surprised to see this young female thrust into a group of very macho-looking males. I was also rather obviously not Brazilian, which similarly aroused their curiosity. As usual when faced with a not entirely friendly reception, I decided to keep smiling and just show them what I could do. Very soon, the handsome player standing next to me in the row was helping me with the rhythm and beat, and we were all getting along fine.

Several hours later the exhausted film crew and I left the building. By this time the noise was so intense that all I was conscious of was an endless vibration which consumed every other sensation. Although it was by now 3 am, the rehearsal showed no signs of stopping, but none of us had the stamina to stay through till the dawn or whenever it was the groups would decide that they had had enough. Weekend after weekend, evening after evening through the year, the *samba* groups rehearse their performance; only to begin all over again as soon as the Parade is through.

My costume was a matter of some importance. The *bateria* would be dressed in *Cabuçu* blue and white, with an extravagant feathered headdress that was to lurch precariously above my eyebrows throughout the Parade. Every detail had to be right or else the judges would have cause to penalize the school, and the outfit was made for me in Rio to make sure that it conformed exactly to the school's requirements. However, there were also plans for me to be moved halfway through the procession on to a float. In the event, this wasn't possible as it would have meant having somehow or other to change costume in the middle of the Parade, and then being smuggled on to the float, all of which could well have lost points for the school. The idea was abandoned, not, however, before my costume for the float had caused considerable inconvenience.

Part of the costume consisted of a pair of long silver leather boots which reached to my thighs. These were made for me in London to make sure they fitted really snugly, and were kept in shape by enormous wooden blocks which fitted inside the boots. As a result, they had to be carried everywhere, off the plane, through customs, into the van that took us into Rio, and through the elegant swing doors of the hotel. The sight of a foreigner lugging about what were obviously part of a *Carnaval* costume caused considerable interest and comment, and I was relieved to have the wretched things safely stashed away in the wardrobe in my room. The rest of the float attire was to be a kind of leotard with a cape over it. The poor woman who made it was responsible for producing a number of outfits and had obviously not slept for days; her eyes were black holes and she was thin as a rake. I was sorry that her trouble had been for nothing, but secretly relieved that I wouldn't have to wear the leotard as it seemed to have been designed for somebody who wasn't at all my shape!

One of the great pleasures of the trip was joining in street bands. I could walk along the street and if I saw a band, stand alongside and join them. It was excellent practice in establishing the *samba* rhythm and as soon as the group realized that I could play, there were no problems about joining in. People would stop and watch, some would dance, and others took photos when they saw a foreign girl playing with what were usually male musicians. It was terrific. I had also hoped to be able to spend more time at the *favelas* to meet the locals and have some sessions with them. This didn't happen, sadly, but it's an ambition for next time I go to Rio.

By the night of the Parade for my *samba* school, I was feeling confident that I would not disgrace my fellow *tamborim* players. I changed into my costume at the hotel, and put on lashings of bronze makeup so that I looked Brazilian. When we arrived at the beginning of the Parade, we discovered chaos. Each school had its own patch milling with performers, and the floats had also to be organized. Timing was everything, and the schools had to follow one another in strict succession and cover the route within the time limit allocated, which meant that some of the less well-rehearsed groups would have to rush or slow the tempo. None of this would escape the judges. The *bateria* were arranged in rows, so again we had to make sure we didn't straggle and kept perfect time. All this and keep the headdress on! I felt as though my neck was frozen by the end of our extended stroll.

The Parade was a tremendous experience, over an hour of playing and walking with crowds of people looking on, cheering and dancing to the *samba* beat. There is a huge grandstand, the *sambodrómo*, which seats 60,000 spectators. Those who can't afford a seat line the route, shouting and cheering like nothing I've ever experienced. The grandstand looms high above the procession and when I saw all those people, tier upon tier, my mouth just opened in a giant 'Oh!' I couldn't believe it. The judges have binoculars so that they can check nothing is being done amiss, and as I passed by I kept my eyes straight ahead, trying to look like any Brazilian *samba* player, although I was also keen that people should be aware I was a girl. This was difficult, given the crush and the obscuring headdress.

Afterwards, I changed out of my costume and stayed with Chris and the film crew to watch some of the other schools, but in the end it was all just too much; we went back to the hotel and collapsed. The Parade continued through the night, the ghostly shapes of the revellers flickering across my television screen until I fell into bed, when *samba* rhythms haunted my dreams.

When I came back to London, I recognized that Rio had marked a turning point. I had a new sense of openness and freedom, an awareness that there was more to music – and to life – than a strict attention to the marks on paper. False notes no longer seemed of serious concern; what was important was to express how I felt about things here and now, and to communicate this feeling in a way that was uninhibited, honest and joyous. This new quality – of spontaneity, relaxation, allowing my intuition to guide me as I played – has stayed with me and continues to influence both my playing and my attitude to life in general. It has also confirmed my belief in the importance of seeking out new challenges if I want to keep growing as a musician. There are so many enriching experiences to be discovered, and it's up to me to find them out and in every way possible to share them with my friends and public. Looking forward, that is one of my major aims.

23

Rhythm song

'Let your deafness no longer be a secret –
even in art.'

Ludwig van Beethoven

The trip to Brazil in February and the subsequent screening of the *South Bank Show* late in the year were not the only outstanding events of 1989. My Prom recital in June was a particular landmark, but this was also the year when I recorded my first solo album *Rhythm Song*.

The idea of a recording contract had been in the air for some time even before I met Jasper Parrott in the spring of 1987. Both EMI and RCA had expressed an interest, and negotiations with RCA had made considerable progress when I was still working with Kaye Artists, but the temporary hiatus without a manager in 1987 had meant that plans were postponed for a while. However, Jasper saw a recording contract as essential to my gaining an international public, particularly in Japan and the United States which both offer good opportunities for musicians. We were also keen to secure a long-term contract not just a one-off, so that I would have a chance to establish a name and build on the success that we hoped my first release would engender. Talks were resumed with RCA and finally we were able to make firm plans for my first solo album.

I was not an absolute beginner where records were concerned. I had started young with *Ellon Academy:*

One, a recording of the school orchestra and concert band which was made in 1979 for local distribution. Cults Percussion Ensemble also made a record, featuring such golden favourites as Ron Forbes' *Autun Carillon* and *Circles*. Later there was the recording at Henry Wood Hall of the Vačkář Concerto for Trumpet with John Wallace for Nimbus Records, and I worked with The Wallace Collection ensemble on a collection of marches by the American composer, John Philip Sousa, popularly known as 'the March King', for Nimbus Records. The cream of all these ventures was the Bartók Sonata for Two Pianos and Percussion with CBS. My sessions work with *Highway* also meant that I was familiar with studio conditions and techniques. What I hadn't yet done was planned and performed my own solo collection.

Once the long-term contract with RCA had been agreed, the next step was to plan the style and repertoire of my first recording. The producer, Ralph Mace, and I decided to choose a variety of short pieces that would have a broad appeal, rather than focusing on any more heavyweight work. *Rhythm Song* was recorded during two groups of sessions in May and September 1989 at the CBS studios in Whitfield Street. On the first day I took a cab to arrive early for a chat with Ralph and the engineer Mike Ross.

The first thing Ralph said to me was, 'I saw you on television last night.' I had been on *Songs of Praise* for a few minutes. Then he said, 'Oh yes – and on *Mastermind*!' Apparently there had been a question about what instruments I played. I was amused to find myself famous for these two slightly incongruous reasons and that quickly broke the ice, and Ralph's approach was very relaxed, trying things out just to see how they would go with no pressure on time. Ralph had worked with James Galway as well as many other musicians, and was used to the idea of a 'serious' musician recording lighter, more popular music, and I

found him marvellous to work with, sensitive, responsive and dedicated. I felt lucky to have both him and
Mike with me on my first solo effort.

The National Philharmonic Orchestra attended the
September sessions where a full orchestra was required,
and there were also a number of other session musicians
involved. Barry Wordsworth, a very charming and
genial conductor with whom I had worked at the Barbican Summer Pops that same year, conducted most of
the orchestral pieces, and I was glad to renew our
acquaintance. Barry has a wonderful feel for the audience and encouraged everyone to hum the well-known
Toreador's Song from Bizet's *Carmen* Suite when we
played it at the Barbican. He looked very mischievous
and comical doing this, and the audience adored him.

The several days of recording went very well. Unlike
my *Highway* sessions, I was working in a huge studio
so had no sense of being cut off or restricted, and the
fact I could move around freely made me perform more
openly, so that I hope there is a sense on the record of
there being a live performer in action. One thing that
particularly pleased me was that we were able to lay
down both *Michi* and Rhythm Song on the first recording. So often pieces have to be played three or four
times and are then cut about and matched together to
get the best effect, which I find artificial, so it was good
to be able to play these very emotional pieces straight
through and know that the final result will be just as I
felt it at the time.

On the last days I stayed to see the tracks being
mixed. It is almost unheard of for performers to do
this, but I was anxious to see how everything was done
and to make sure that the effects I had been aiming
for received full attention. Both Mike and Ralph were
receptive to this and we had a wonderful time working
together. I have a very good memory for what I have
played, so was able to discuss with them any doubts or
reservations I had about how the sound might have

come out. Afterwards I felt that my first record had turned out just as I had hoped and was worth the long gestation period.

In particular I was happy about the selection of works we had agreed should be included. We had put a lot of thought into exploring what would be the best balance of items in the recording, which, unlike a recital, is intended to be listened to as a continuous stream of sound, and to be played time and time again. What would give the maximum enjoyment to the listener, what kind of atmosphere did we want and how best should we establish it? Should all the pieces suggest a similar response, a series of exciting fireworks, for instance, to create an energetic mood, or all romantic pieces; or should we try to vary the mood and tempo? I found these questions fascinating, and naturally had plenty of my own ideas about what the repertoire should be. The pieces we finally selected were all favourites with me, demonstrating a range of instruments and techniques, with lots of opportunity for razzmatazz and some depth of feeling.

I look forward to developing this aspect of my work, following up with serious contemporary works and concertos among others. One ambition is to record the old-time xylophone solos that used to be played at the beginning of the century. They are barely considered now, but are foot-tapping ragtime pieces, which would be terrific accompaniments to dancing – tap and jazz ballet and musicals.

Apart from recording, and filming for the *South Bank Show*, my schedule was increasingly crowded with performances. A feature writer recently described me as having over one hundred professional bookings a year; this may or may not be accurate – I haven't had time to count! My life does get busier and busier, although it would be difficult to explain exactly how I spend my time. 'Describe a typical week,' people sometimes ask me, but the answer has to be 'No week is the same.'

Certainly no year of my professional life has born any resemblance to the previous twelve months; the only common factor is that every day is jampacked with people, places and music. When I think back to my childhood I find it hard to remember what happened at any particular time, as the years flowed into one another, an endlessly repeating pattern of similar events. Now the problem is quite different; every few days the kaleidoscope of my life seems to be shaken anew, and the pieces fall together into different but equally intriguing patterns. A brief look at some of the year's events may indicate its variety:

January Profile in *The Scotsman* PERSPECTIVE 89 series; *Highway* session; shopping for Brazil; guest appearance with Northern Sinfonia in Newcastle, Stockton, and Scarborough; recording with Scottish Chamber Orchestra for *The Ghost of Faffner Hall*, a children's television programme; travel to Brazil for the *South Bank Show* documentary.

February Brazil; *Highway* session; The Piccolo Pack, a concert for children with the Scottish Chamber Orchestra in Edinburgh; interview for *Songs of Praise*; to Ireland for concert with Ulster Symphony Orchestra, which was televised with inserts of me presenting instruments from the percussion family used in the programme; Glasgow for concert with St Bride's Chamber Orchestra; concerts in Glasgow, Edinburgh and Aberdeen for Scottish Chamber Orchestra's fifteenth anniversary: Feld's *Fantasie Concertante* for Flute, Percussion and Strings with James Galway; *Highway* session; Grammy Award for the Bartók recording with Sir Georg Solti and Murray Perahia.

March More *Highway* sessions, which go on

through the year; Royal Scottish Academy of Music and Drama in Glasgow for master classes and lunch time recital; interviews, photo session; lots of practice for future engagements.

April Filming with Chris Hunt for *South Bank Show*; practising for record; master class at Rugby Girls' School; return to Leamington Hastings for a recital.

May Recording *Rhythm Song*; Prom press conference; Brighton Festival concert at Lancing College Chapel with the Amadeus Chamber Orchestra of Poland; interview with Michael Berkeley for Radio 4's *Kaleidoscope* arts programme, discussing my work as a percussionist and focusing on Bartók's Sonata for Two Pianos and Percussion; recital in Edinburgh at Royal Scottish Academy.

June Belgium for Sir Yehudi Menuhin Live Music Now concert at Ancienne Belgique in Brussels; Orkney for my own Celebrity Recital at St Magnus Festival; concert at Harrow Leisure Centre; recital at Ellon Academy; recital at St Kane's Church, New Deer; concert at Dornoch Cathedral near Inverness; concert for Dulwich Choral Society; Lamp of Lothian recitals.

July Recitals in Holloway Prison and Wormwood Scrubs Prison; appeared on John Dunn radio show, *People* programme, *Newsbeat*; Breakfast TV, Sky television; radio and magazine interviews; recital for City of London Festival at Cripplegate Church; Promenade recital at Kensington Town Hall.

August Interview with National Broadcasting Corporation; talking to Richard Rodney Bennett about the concerto he is writing for me; Latin American Fiesta concert at the Barbican with the London Symphony Orchestra for the Summer Pops; recording with the LSO for Decca's CD video of our Pops programme.

September   Finish recording and editing *Rhythm Song*; concert at St Martin-in-the-Fields for *Marchioness* disaster fund (the pleasure boat that sank on the Thames with many young lives lost); charity concert at the Mansion House in London; Omagh Festival in Ireland.

October   Cricklade Festival; recital at Sheldonian Theatre, Oxford; recital in Coventry; recital at Cranleigh School; concert with the Scottish Chamber Orchestra in Kirkcaldy (there was a Chicago theatre impresario in the audience who was keen to know more about me!); present prizes at Mary Hare Grammar School for the Deaf prizegiving ceremony; Saturday morning children's concert in Salisbury; photo session, and the Les Dawson show for television; Beethoven Fund Ball Appeal for The Elizabeth Foundation; children's concert at the Theatre Royal in Winchester; concert with the Royal Air Force Band; Concert at London College of Music, the London premiere of Sallinen's 2nd Symphony, working on my autobiography.

November   I win a Junior Chamber International Award as one of ten Outstanding Young Persons of the World; to Nashville for Pasic '89, where I perform the US premiere of John McCleod's Concerto for Percussion with the Nashville Symphony Orchestra – my own concerto debut in the USA; meet BMG/RCA in New York to discuss future albums; record *Michi* for Tony Palmer's film *The Children*; to Stavanger in Norway for concert with the Stavanger Symphony Orchestra, conducted by Avi Ostrovsky; master class and concert at the Rogaland Musikkonservatorium, and travel to Helsinki in Finland; screening of the *South Bank Show* documentary on my visit to Brazil.

December Concert with Finnish Radio Symphony Orchestra; concert for AIDS with the Helsinki Philharmonic Orchestra; master classes at Royal Scottish Academy of Music and Drama; concert for Sir Malcolm Sargent Cancer Fund; audition fourteen percussionists for the Young Musician of the Year Percussion master class to be held in January and televised in February; working with Howard Blake on a concerto he is writing for me; *Daytime Live* interview in Birmingham; interview with Grampian Television: 'Out of the '80s'; sitting for my portrait with the Hon. Mrs Honour Earl; Hanover for *Nase Varn*, live television programme broadcast to all German-speaking countries (my suitcase was lost in transit, so I had a mad dash round Hanover buying a suitable outfit to appear on the show!); informed that I have been voted Scotswoman of the Decade by readers of *The Scotsman* and viewers of Scottish Television, interview at Grampian studios.

One event that was particularly welcome was the opportunity to discuss Bartók's Sonata for Two Pianos and Percussion with Michael Berkeley in the forty-minute interview for Radio 4's *Kaleidoscope*. Not only did we talk about the Bartók, I had a marimba, snare drum, cymbals, Brazilian and other small instruments in the studio, and was able to demonstrate some of the effects that I particularly admire.

The concert with the Ulster Orchestra in Belfast was

another high point. It was recorded for television and I was invited to present some of the percussion instruments used in the performance in a special introduction. The works performed were the Russian composer Rodion Shchedrin's unusual arrangement of Bizet's *Carmen* Suite for percussion and strings and Miyoshi's Concerto for Marimba and Strings with John Lubbock conducting. I made the television introduction relaxed and informal, wearing a rather snazzy T-shirt and trousers, and having some fun demonstrating the different sounds of a whole range of instruments, not forgetting a giant tam-tam: 'I just can't resist . . . Bong!!!' The sound could resonate for ever if I didn't damp it down between my palms.

For the Summer Pops at the Barbican with the London Symphony Orchestra, I wore a delicious pink silk dress with a full skirt and a tiny bolero top that I was glad to be able to remove as the tempo hotted up. Under Barry Wordsworth's lively direction I played the *Carmen* Suite again, and works by the young Brazilian composer Ney Rosauro. His Concerto for Marimba and Strings was completed in 1986 and unusually has four movements: greeting, lament, a dance and farewell. It is a piece of many contrasts, ending with a sizzling finale which the audience responded to with enthusiasm. The *Braziliana* is a short percussion solo from Rosauro's *Cenas Amerindias*, and has a rather remarkable tocking background like the insides of an old grandfather clock. It requires meticulous balance and timing to overlay this rhythmic beat with layers of melodic figures. Again the audience were delighted, and the *Daily Mail* critic Tully Potter also seemed to enjoy the fun. 'Miss Glennie . . . bashed about on a further collection of strange objects,' he wrote somewhat inelegantly, while 'the LSO and Barry Wordsworth sat as mesmerised as the audience'.

Festivals continued to be rewarding and full of pleasant surprises, and to attract gratifying interest from both the public and critics. The review in the *Wiltshire and Gloucestershire Standard* of my recital at the Cricklade Festival expressed an appreciation of the marimba that was deeply satisfying. 'The musical range of the marimba is quite astonishing,' it read, 'from the obvious percussive sounds to those more closely associated with the organ.' In a musical environment that still sometimes reacts with suspicion and prejudice to percussion instruments, this kind of sensitive regard is very welcome.

Another kind of appreciation came after I received the Junior Chamber International award as one of ten Outstanding Young Persons of the World. All kinds of people whom I had met sent me cards and messages of congratulation. Unfortunately I was in Nashville at the time of the award ceremony, but we managed to arrange for my mother to collect it on my behalf, and both my parents attended the dinner in Birmingham to mark the event.

The performances in Nashville with the Nashville Symphony Orchestra were great occasions, my first appearance with an American orchestra, and the American premiere of John McLeod's Percussion Concerto. I could hardly move on the stage which was filled to capacity with the array of instruments that John requires for the work. The *Nashville Banner* critic wrote imaginatively, 'Rolling drums and spine-tingling fanfares in the brass section sounded like trumpeting elephants stampeding across the plains.' He praised the 'rare diversity' of the composition, with its percussive influences from the Far East, Malaysia, Africa, the Caribbean and American jazz. 'Throughout the five movements Glennie moved gracefully from one instrument to another producing delicate shadings and intense thunders with equal ease. It was a display of rare talent.' Daniel Roumain in the *Vaunderbilt University Hustler* was also impressed: 'the barefoot Glennie . . . handle[d] each phrase with delicacy and complete musical understanding, . . . she also seemed to be in complete control of the orchestra.' We had rapturous applause from the audience, and John was there to take a bow; a very exciting and gratifying response to the work he had created especially for me.

Another exciting trip abroad was the visit to Scandinavia to appear with the Stavanger Symphony Orchestra in Norway, and the Finnish Radio Symphony Orchestra and the Finnish Philharmonic Orchestra. This was an exciting and unusual opportunity to work with different conductors and orchestras, and to play four percussion concertos in the space of twelve days: Miyoshi's Concerto for Marimba and Strings, Milhaud's Concerto for Percussion and Small Orchestra and Concerto for Marimba, Vibraphone and Orchestra, and the American composer Fisher Tull's Dialogues for Solo Percussion and Orchestra. 'Evelyn Glennie was really astonishing,' wrote the Finnish reviewer; 'she played with rhythmic intensity and a sensitive feel for dynamics.' The eclectic origins of the Tull – jazz, liturgical music, Bach, Hindemith and Bartók – aroused appreciative comment, as did my ability to handle its swinging rhythms as well as 'the most skilful jazz drummer'. I enjoyed the trip with its responsive audiences, and the opportunity to play music in a truly international way.

The year ended with the marvellous accolade of being voted Scotswoman of the Decade by readers of *The Scotsman* and viewers of Scottish Television. Sir James Black, who was awarded the Nobel Prize for Medicine in 1988 and had pioneered the development of betablockers for the treatment of heart disease, was Scotsman of the Decade, and I was pleased and honoured to be coupled with so distinguished a fellow Scot for this award. I had in fact met Sir James at Ronnie Cass's house for dinner some months previously. Ronnie likes to tell the story of how Sir James talked away about scientific matters, and I nodded and smiled and put in a word or two, looking very intelligent. 'My goodness,' he thought, 'is she a brilliant scientist as well as a musician?' After a while Ronnie and I began to talk about music, and Sir James was quick to point out that we were talking over his head. 'I know that,' I replied with a cheeky smile, 'I'm just getting my own back!'

Margaret Moodie, the chairwoman of the Scottish Association for the Deaf, generously wrote to me after I had won the award to say that I was an inspiration, not only to those who could enjoy my music, but also to people who were deaf or had impaired hearing and didn't have access to music in the normal way. If I have been an inspiration, I am delighted; if I can encourage others to believe in their ability to overcome difficulties and to go for what they want, it is a great joy, and I feel privileged to be in a position where I am able to communicate with so many people, to let them share my optimism about life's possibilities.

24

Good Vibrations

I began this book by thinking about my personal history, the story of how my life had developed from my quiet and happy childhood on a farm in rural Aberdeenshire to the moment when I stood on the stage at Kensington Town Hall, receiving the standing ovation that had greeted the first solo percussion recital ever to have been given at the BBC's Henry Wood Promenade Concerts. So much has happened in a comparatively short time, and I have already achieved some of my dearest ambitions as far as percussion is concerned. But there is no question of sitting back and feeling that I have 'arrived'. There is still so much to be achieved and developed, both as a musician and to give percussion the prominence it deserves in the musical world. The events of 1989 seem in many ways to be the beginning of my career rather than any kind of culmination, and when I look towards the future I find it difficult to make predictions. Anything might happen, but my aim is the same as it always has been: to make music to the best of my ability and to communicate my delight in it to audiences of every kind all over the world.

I remember telling Terry O'Reilly when we were working together on *A Will to Win*, 'All I want is a chance – to prove that I can make it as a solo percussionist.' *Good Vibrations* is the story of how I created and took that chance, but I couldn't have done it without my family and friends and all the other people who have helped and encouraged me along the way, with letters and money and flowers and applause. This book is not just about me; it is also a tribute and my personal thank you to all the people, named and anonymous, who appear in its pages.

Index